THE GNOSTICS

Andrew Phillip Smith is the editor of *The Gnostic* magazine and the author of several books on Gnosticism and early Christianity: *Gnostic Writings on the Soul, The Lost Sayings of Jesus* and *The Gospel of Philip*. He also runs a small publishing company, Bardic Press, publishing reprints and niche works in the areas of Gnosticism and early Christianity, Celtic interest, Gurdjieff/Fourth Way and Sufi poetry. Born in Penarth, Wales, he now lives with his family in Dublin.

THE GNOSTICS

HISTORY

TRADITION . SCRIPTURES

INFLUENCE

ANDREW PHILLIP SMITH

WATKINS PUBLISHING

LONDON

This edition published in the UK in 2008 by
Watkins Publishing, Sixth Floor, Castle House,
75–76 Wells Street, London W1T 3QH

1 3 5 7 9 10 8 6 4 2

Designed by Jerry Goldie
Typeset by Dorchester Typesetting Group
Printed and bound in Great Britain

British Library Cataloguing-in-Publication Data Available

ISBN: 978-1-905857-64-7

www.watkinspublishing.co.uk

CONTENTS

For my family

INTRODUCTION

'Ears to hear and eyes to see,
this is the tragic ability of the Gnostic.'

LUPIERI P.35

A God who lies about himself and is not the ultimate divinity that he claims himself to be; a Church that is ignorant of the nature of its own God; lost gospels that were suppressed by the Orthodoxy; a reality that is not what it appears to be, and is controlled by malign authorities; the secret knowledge of the true nature of our world – these are all Gnostic themes that have reappeared in modern novels and films such as Philip Pullman's *His Dark Materials* trilogy, Dan Brown's *The Da Vinci Code* and *The Matrix*. Philip Pullman's trilogy draws on the ideas of the ancient Gnostics and the writings of William Blake in its vision of a mind-controlling Church and of a diminished false God who is neither the absolute ruler of the universe nor even its fundamental spiritual principle.

The Da Vinci Code uses the Gnostic gospels to present an alternative history of Christianity in which Jesus had been the partner of Mary Magdalene, a history which, according to Brown, was suppressed by the paternalistic, masculine Church.

In *The Matrix*, the protagonist Neo discovers that his reality is in fact an illusion controlled and manipulated by hidden rulers – the Machines – that are opposed to humanity and use the human race for their own purposes.

In the twentieth and twenty-first centuries, the archaeological discovery of ancient Gnostic manuscripts has opened a window into the world of the Gnostic sects. Not only are many of these writings available again for the first time since the fourth century, but our culture has proved itself to be well suited to receive the influence of Gnosticism. Our multi-cultural, fragmented, somewhat post-religious world has much in common with the early centuries of the Common Era, during which Gnosticism was born and thrived. The central tenets of Gnosticism – that we humans are somehow asleep to our lives and to the true meaning of reality, and yet can awaken; that there is a higher form of personal religion in comparison with which organized religion is a travesty; that reality is not what it seems to be – have spread into diverse forms of popular culture. Yet the history and the literature of the Gnostics themselves are still obscure to most people.

What did they write, and how can we understand their writings? What did they believe about essential religious concepts such as God, the soul and the body, or about sexuality? Did they accept the early Catholic Church or were they the sworn enemies of ecclesiastical organization? Were they heretics or an entirely separate movement? Were they completely wiped out by Orthodox Christianity, or did Gnosticism survive?

We shall see that even though certain aspects of the origins and history of the Gnostics are obscure, we now have plenty of information on their varied views of the world. Although Gnostic movements have been battered both by the winds of time and the spiritual warfare of Christian Orthodoxy, even today there still survives a traditional religious group that is directly descended from the ancient Gnostics. Once the ideas of Gnosticism had been sown into the world, they could never be completely oppressed, and Gnostic concepts keep pushing to the surface in both religious and secular contexts in the Western world.

The Gnostics did not subscribe to a central ecclesiastical authority, and they were relentlessly creative with their mythology, continuing to rework and rewrite it, so there is no single definitive version of the Gnostic myth and there are no official Gnostic scriptures. Gnosticism poses – and perhaps answers – questions that are fundamental to human existence. Who is the real God, and how can we know him (or her) directly? Why is there evil in the world? Does established, organized religion really point to the truth?

The original ancient Gnostics were Christian-related sects who are known mostly through their own writings, which use myth and spiritual metaphor and often turn the stories of the Bible upside down. We also possess the polemics of their enemies, the heresy-hunting Church Fathers who, in their attempts to refute the Gnostics, preserved much information on them.

The Gnostics were distinguished from other early Christians in their emphasis on *gnosis*, the Greek word for 'knowledge', rather than faith; according to the Gnostics, it is gnosis itself that saves, redeems, and provides liberation. Conventional Christianity emphasizes faith in Christ, in his crucifixion and res-urrection and his status as the son of God, the saviour and redeemer of humanity, at the centre of its religion. The Gnostics also saw Jesus as a saviour and redeemer, but their Jesus saved and redeemed by bringing *knowledge* of the universe and man's true place within it. The knowledge that he brought could teach mankind how to liberate the seed of spiritual light that was hidden within, and enable humanity to know the true God.

Gnosis is a direct kind of knowledge, more akin to the way in which one knows another person than to intellectual or factual knowledge, and might be translated alternatively as 'acquaintance' or 'recognition'. True gnosis is a direct knowledge of the Self and the truth about the universe. Knowledge of oneself becomes knowledge of God, because the deepest and highest part of us is akin to the divine. The concept of gnosis may initially seem mysterious, but it is connected to the modern spiritual and psychological concept of consciousness. The word 'consciousness' derives from the Latin *conscius*, 'sharing knowledge with', a word that is cognate with the Greek *gnosis*.

Consciousness is knowledge of oneself, or awareness of oneself, and some spiritual writers have coined terms like self-consciousness (not in the ordinary English sense of embarrassment), superconsciousness or objective consciousness to clarify the difference between our ordinary everyday consciousness and spiritually higher states of consciousness.

Most people have experienced a waking up or coming to at moments in their lives. Perhaps it occurred in childhood, or perhaps it was experienced as an adult in connection with some unusual or intense situation – a quietness or a strangeness, a different sense of oneself, accompanied by an awareness of one's surroundings and perhaps a feeling of *knowing*, however fleetingly, the truth about one's true self and the world. The experience may be simply a unitive state or may be accompanied by visions. These states of higher consciousness demand explanation, and the Gnostic teachings provide us with a meaningful intellectual structure that explains life on earth, and also provides techniques by which we might experience these moments of illumination once again. This is gnosis – the direct experience of higher reality and of the divine self, accompanied by knowledge of what is being experienced, the importance of the experience, and its relationship to the rest of the universe.

* * *

The ancient Gnostics drew a clear line between the material world and the spiritual world of gnosis. Gnosticism is thus dualistic. There is spirit and there is matter. There is the material world and there is the world of the spirit, often called the *Pleroma*, from a Greek word meaning 'fullness' or 'completeness'. To many, this dualism may initially seem to be surprising, being perceived as a quality that belongs more to fundamentalist religion than to true spirituality, reminiscent of the importance that many fundamentalist Churches give to the influence of Satan in this world, which thus turns the world into a moral battleground between Christianity and the forces of evil. But classical Gnostic dualism was a dualism within unity. All and everything springs forth from God, but the material world is a result of a cosmic fall, an error made in the lowest reaches of the spiritual realm.

Matter is the crudest and lowest aspect of the universe, and it is of matter that our bodies are formed. But the creation of mankind could not proceed without a spark of the spiritual realm residing in each human. We humans therefore have a duality of matter and spirit within us. We respond to base matter, but we have divine spirits, in which our true identities reside. Ultimately, everything is contained within the divine, even the base physical world, and it is only in our ignorance (lack of gnosis) that there appears to be duality.

But this world of matter did not come into existence through a mechanical process or by chance. The Gnostics, like the Christians and Jews, thought that the world had been created by God. The Gnostics even agreed that the creator God was the same as the God of the Christians and Jews. However, the Gnostics felt that this God was an arrogant and ignorant abortion, truly a jealous God, a despot who knew nothing of the spiritual realm above him. Thus mainstream religion worshipped the wrong God, and the real God could be known through gnosis, not through any conventional doctrine or belief.

All of these ideas were expressed through the medium of myth, not through philosophy or strict dogma. Gnostic myths come in several flavours, but the mythic framework usually involves a description of the higher realm and an explanation of the fall that occurred, followed by an account of the possibility of salvation and restoration.

Until the discovery of the Nag Hammadi Library, we had only the hostile accounts of the early Church Fathers along with a few original texts which either represented a late stage of Gnosticism or in any case had not received enough scholarly attention.

It was in December 1945 that the Nag Hammadi codices were discovered. Mohammed Ali es-Samman and his brother Khalifah Ali, two Arab camel drivers, were out looking for fertilizer at the bottom of the high chalk cliff of Djebel-el-Tarif. They found a large earthenware jar, which they smashed open, slightly wary of what they might find, only to discover 12 books. (One of the books had another pamphlet bound into it, so the books are now numbered as being 13 in total.)

These are codices, not scrolls. Scrolls are continuous sheets rolled up rather like rolls of wallpaper, but a codex is a manuscript book copied by hand before the invention of printing, but bound in essentially the same way as the modern book. The pages of the codices are made from papyrus cut into sheets and bound between covers. The covers of the Nag Hammadi codices are of leather and have a clasp extending from the back to the front, so that they resemble a modern briefcase. All of the Nag Hammadi codices are written in the Coptic language, which is the final form of the ancient Egyptian language, by which stage it was written in Greek letters instead of hieroglyphs or demotic script, with a few extra letters to represent sounds that are lacking in the Greek language. As far as we know the original language of every single text in the collection was Greek.

After their discovery, these codices eventually made their way into the hands of scholars, often through particularly circuitous routes. The journey of the tomes was complicated when the brothers who had found the manuscripts took revenge on the man who had killed their father and had to go into hiding. The books were left with a Coptic priest whose brother, having some notion of their potential sales price, sold a volume to a Cairo antiques dealer. Through a variety of sales, attempted sales and smugglings, the entire collection was ultimately preserved at the Cairo Museum. The 12 (or 13) codices contain a wealth of Gnostic and related literature, including the now well-known *Gospel of Thomas* and *Gospel of Philip*.

The *Gospel of Judas*, made famous in 2006 by the promotional efforts of its publishers *National Geographic*, had a similarly tortured history. The initial discovery of the *Gospel of Judas* is unknown to us, but it is quite likely that it was discovered in an Egyptian tomb. The subsequent turbulent history of what is now called Codex Tchacos, after Frieda Tchacos who sold the volume to National Geographic, or, to those who dislike National Geographic's claim of ownership, Codex Judas, is now fairly well documented, and described in Chapter 3.

Codex Tchacos contains four separate texts, each of which is damaged to a greater or lesser extent, but it is the *Gospel of Judas* which has taken the limelight. Pride of place in the newly discovered Gnostic gospel is given to Judas Iscariot, but his significance in the gospel is still being debated by academics and others. Judas may be the hero of the story, by means of a revolutionary technique named inverse exegesis, which turned the conventional biblical interpretations upside down and was used by the Gnostics as a new way of reading scripture, or he may simply be portrayed as the archetypal disciple – like the other disciples in the *Gospel of Judas*, a traitor and a worshipper of the wrong God. However the academic discussion might play out, the *Gospel of Judas* is full of Gnostic teaching.

* * *

The Gnostics first appeared in the first centuries of the Common Era, in the context of eastern Mediterranean Hellenistic civilization. The earliest recorded Gnostics were people like Menander, Satornilos, Basilides and – perhaps the earliest of all, if he was not merely a legend – Simon Magus. At the peak of Gnostic activity, there were many different groups, given outlandish names by the Church Fathers like the Marcosians, Ophites, Cainites, Naasenes, Carpocratians and the Borborites, but modern scholars usually divide them into two categories – Sethians and Valentinians. The Gnostics themselves probably just called themselves Christians. The Sethians were probably the earlier of the two branches and trace themselves back to the mythical Seth in the book of Genesis, whereas the Valentinians take their name from the historical Gnostic teacher Valentinus.

At times, the Gnostics seemed like strong competitors to mainstream Christianity, but they lost out as the stranglehold of Christian Orthodoxy tightened its grip. When Emperor Constantine converted to Christianity and removed the restrictions on Christian worship, Christianity reacted to its wider acceptance by codifying and standardizing its dogma and forms of worship and stiffening its resolve against heterodox Christian groups like the Gnostics. It is perhaps no accident the Nag Hammadi codices were compiled at roughly the same time that apocryphal literature was being condemned.

But the ancient Sethian and Valentinian Gnostics had their successors and their relatives. There is currently much academic discussion over the definition of Gnosticism, and over which Christian groups qualify as Gnostic and whether the Gnostics even called themselves Gnostic. In the current work I shall not be too concerned about definition, and I shall consider Gnosticism as a loose network of related ideas, texts, groups and individuals. If the religion of the second-century heterodox Christian Marcion lacks reference to gnosis itself (and I do not feel that he is truly a Gnostic as such), his movement is nevertheless strongly dualistic and related to Gnosticism. If the Manichaean religion, now dead but once widespread in Asia and parts of Europe, tended towards belief and practice rather than gnosis, the Manichaeans' myths, dualism and repeated references to gnosis are nonetheless Gnostic. And so on with the Cathars and Paulicians and Bogomils. A historical chain links all of these to the ancient Gnostics, as is also the case with the Mandaeans, the sole surviving Gnostic religion, now threatened by the current war in Iraq.

Other spiritual systems have Gnostic qualities to them – for instance, Advaita Vedanta, Mahayana Buddhism, Kabbalah, Neoplatonism and certain forms of Islamic mysticism. Not all of these necessarily have any historical relationship to the ancient Christian Gnostics, but may have arrived independently to similar conclusions. The late scholar of Gnosticism Ioan Couliano proposed that Gnosticism constitutes an intellectual system which, like other systems, has a limited number of options, a limited number of binary switches that may be turned on or off. There are only so many ways in which issues such as life after death, the existence of God, or the relationship of spirit to physical matter can be treated, and thus similar solutions keep recurring.

Once the Gnostic myth and Gnostic concepts had appeared in the world, they existed henceforth as a kind of ideal form. To move beyond a mere academic application of this idea, we might say that once the seeds of a Gnostic viewpoint had been sown into the world (which probably happened in the first or at the latest second century CE) it could then find a multitude of expressions. Even if the historical continuity of Gnostic teachings were to be terminated (and it was when the medieval Cathars were persecuted and slaughtered), the ideas would still exist and could be fanned back into a flame. Thus someone like William Blake, who could only have had the slightest exposure to Gnostic ideas, was able to come up with a genuinely Gnostic system by himself. And the discovery of the Nag Hammadi Library, and other Gnostic literature, made the ideas again available to humanity so they could take root in the human heart and once again produce gnosis.

* * *

So, what can we gain by exploring the Gnostics? We can receive an alternative view of the world and of our place within it. We can explore forms of Christianity that were lost and are perhaps more applicable to our current lives than traditional Christianity. We can revive forgotten traditions, understand lost myths and teaching. But most importantly, we may experience gnosis ourselves.

CHAPTER 1

THE STORY OF GOD: GNOSTIC MYTHOLOGY

'But since they differ so widely among themselves both as respects doctrine and tradition, and since those of them who are recognized as being most modern make it their effort daily to invent some new opinion, and to bring out what no one ever before thought of, it is a difficult matter to describe all their opinions.'

IRENAEUS

The main mode of expression of the Gnostics was literature, and their literature survives in a small number of limited forms. A brief perusal of the Nag Hammadi Library reveals a few concise texts which consist mostly of sayings or dialogues – and it is no accident that those more straightforward texts like the *Gospel of Thomas* and the *Gospel of Philip* have had the widest appeal since the rediscovery of the codices – but the majority of the Nag Hammadi texts are complex, sprawling mythical creations.

Despite the popular designation of the Nag Hammadi texts as 'Gnostic gospels', the gospel form as an account of the earthly life of Jesus was not generally favoured by Gnostics. They valued Jesus as a redeemer, a revealer of knowledge whose death was not of central importance to his mission. Rather, Gnostic texts typically, but not exclusively, describe and utilize the Gnostic myth of the creation of the world and humanity and all that led up to it and proceeded from it. The Gnostics, in all their incarnations (Manichaeans, Mandaeans and Cathars in addition to the ancient Gnostics) have consistently turned to myth as being the best vehicle for expressing their insights into mankind and the universe.

A myth can encapsulate essential meaning in a story, can express archetypal truths about man and the world through the interplay of its characters. Myths are non-dogmatic and can be subject to endless interpretation and re-interpretation. The Gnostics did not invent their own myths from scratch (though there is much that occurs for the first time in Gnostic myth), or use the extensive mythic background of the pagan classical world. Rather, their myths drew on the Bible and particularly, even almost exclusively, on the book of Genesis. Genesis was a rich vein of material with its vivid sketches of creation and fall and its alluring, condensed tales of the patriarchs, and is still the best-known book in the Old Testament.

The only problem that the Gnostics had with the Bible was that they didn't agree with it. Yet their disagreement led neither to a search for some other source of myth, nor to a simple rejection of God or religion, but to a creative engagement with the Hebrew myths. The Gnostics turned the Bible on its head: they made biblical heroes into tools of the evil demiurge; they made obscure characters into redeemers of humanity; and they made God, the Jewish and Christian deity, into a demon.

Yet the Bible was only one aspect of the cultural background of the Gnostics. They were influenced equally by Plato, but they didn't accept Plato's philosophy lying down, any more than they did the Bible. Plato made good use of myth himself, and the metaphysical aspects of his philosophy were often expressed allusively and poetically, leaving plenty of scope for interpretation and expansion. In the third century Plotinus, the leading Neoplatonist, argued against the Gnostics' adaptation of Plato's philosophy and in particular against their perceived denigration of the material world, but he recognized that the Gnostics were competitors to Platonists as much as they were to Christians. The Gnostic myths represent a meeting of the Hebrew Bible and Platonism, and a response to the intra-national Hellenistic culture, but they are something more than that too. They are a new creation.

It is common enough for scholars of Gnosticism to refer to the 'Gnostic myth' – the central myth of a fall from the spiritual realm that results in the existence of the ignorant creator God who makes this world, the subsequent plight of humanity and the attempts of the spiritual world to enable humans to regain their birthright. And it is tempting to reconstruct an original from which all the later varieties of the Gnostic myth developed. Some of the earliest Gnostic or semi-Gnostic teachers like Satornilos and Basilides had myths that lacked some of the features of what we might call full-blown Gnosticism, but in truth there was never any ideal form of the myth that was later corrupted, or splintered into many forms, never any fundamental expression of an ur-myth; Gnostics were too creative and independent for that.

The variety and diversity of the Gnostic myths show that Gnostics were expected to develop their own personal understandings and to elaborate, re-imagine or alter the myths whenever necessary. There are thus many treatments of the Gnostic myth. Some accounts focus on the mythical history of humankind, some on the grand cosmogony that initiates the story. (Cosmology is the study of the universe as it is; cosmogony the study of the creation of the universe.) Some accounts focus on the fall (which is not the fall of Adam and Eve in the usual interpretations of Genesis, but the fall of Sophia), on how we and the world came to be as we are, others on the possibility of liberation and redemption. In some myths, such as the *Exegesis on the Soul* and the *Hymn of the Pearl*, the soul is the main character, and the story is told without much of a cosmological framework.

The Gnostic myth may be said to have four stages. Firstly there is the production of the Pleroma, the divine realm of spiritual fullness, and the emanation of the various aeons that inhabit it. Next we have the fall of Sophia, the youngest of the aeons. Then the birth of the demiurge and the creation of the material world, and lastly the story of humanity, the creation and development of mankind, and the redeemers and revealers who brought gnosis to the world to help the trapped seeds of light to escape.

As a whole, the myth describes the process by which God emanates to fill the spiritual realm. At its furthest limits, this accidentally creates the material world, in which shards of spirit are trapped. The on-going story is that of humanity's attempts to free the imprisoned light which may then rejoin the Pleroma.

In the beginning there was only God. God may be known directly through gnosis, but he cannot be defined. (My use of the masculine gender to describe God is merely traditional, though the ultimate God is very often considered male, particularly as a father, by the Gnostics.) We can only say what God is not, not what he is, and this negative theology is very characteristic of Gnosticism. Any attempt to label or define God limits him, and therefore cannot express his absolute, transcendent qualities. God is immeasurable, ineffable, unknowable, unnameable. These epithets do not limit God because they express what God is not, rather than what he is.

But God is not completely unapproachable. Without compromising his unity and transcendence, he began to emanate various qualities of himself, characteristics like Mind, Silence, Depth, Love, which are known as aeons. These qualities were formed in male and female pairs, *syzygies*, and male and female mated and produced yet younger aeons, which were further aspects of God. The final quality to be emanated was wisdom, which in the Greek is *Sophia*. God and all of his hypostases or qualities were united together in the fullness of God: the Pleroma.

Sophia, as the last and lowest of the aeons, was not content. She did not rebel against God, as did Lucifer in Christian thought, but her curiosity and desire led her to fall away. Some say that she wished to know God directly but could not reach high enough and so fell lower than the Pleroma, others that in exploring what was beneath her she somehow copulated with nothingness. However events may have developed, Sophia conceived and the resulting child, often referred to cruelly but accurately as an abortion, was a misshapen thing called Ialdabaoth (sometimes named Saklas or Nebruel). Ialdabaoth knew nothing of God or of the great Pleroma above, perhaps not even of his mother, Sophia. Thinking that he was the only God, he created the material world and declared it good. But in comparison with the great eternal qualities of God that comprised the Pleroma, the earth was a shadow, composed of gross matter.

Once created, the living creatures of the earth lived squalid lives, devouring each other and copulating to create more of themselves. Ialdabaoth created the archons, the rulers or authorities, to govern the world and its inhabitants. But despite his arrogance, Ialdabaoth was unable to create the world without some element of his mother Sophia, or of another higher being, entering into it, and hence a small spark of the light of the Pleroma made its way into created beings. As a result, humans have a spark of spirit within them that may be fanned into a flame, a fragment of divinity that can join the whole, a seed of light that can grow.

In some versions of the myth, some of the aeons, the hypostasized qualities of God, are interested in helping humans to develop their spiritual components, to help the seeds of light to grow and to escape their imprisonment in the dark matter of the world. So redeemers have been sent from the Pleroma to bring teachings which illuminate the situation in which mankind finds itself. These teachings can lead to direct acquaintance (gnosis) with the Pleroma. And that is the current state of the world according to the Gnostics.

The above is a simplified version of the Gnostic myth. There is no extant version of the myth that exactly follows this plot, and many of the texts differ considerably in their emphasis and in their details, but the ancient Gnostics would have recognized the above story as being within their tradition.

The literary critic Harold Bloom, who has a high regard for Gnosticism in its broadest sense, wrote a modern Gnostic novel,

The Flight to Lucifer, and has even argued that American religion is Gnostic, developed the concept of 'creative misprision'. According to this theory, new ideas, interpretations and literary creations are often based on a misinterpretation of the original text, whether that false interpretation was deliberate or otherwise. Did Gnostics really believe that the God of the Old Testament was intended to be the evil demiurge? Did they really believe that this was the truth of the Bible, or were they looking for a way in which they could derive meaning from the scriptures of the parent religion, willfully playing around with them in the knowledge that the Gnostic interpretation was 180 degrees away from the conventional interpretation?

The ancients were more at home with myth than we are and the supposed contradictions between literal truth and myth would not have been such a concern to them. Yet we moderns cannot help asking, 'Did they really believe in these myths? Did they think that they were metaphor? Or did they believe in a literal demiurge?'

For centuries the Greek classical tradition had encouraged rational intellectual enquiry into myth, and in Plato's *Phaedrus*, Socrates rejects the myth of Orithya being carried off by Boreas, the north wind, as not having any significance beyond it being the dimly remembered account of a girl having been blown off a cliff. The relativism of the Hellenistic world was the result of the meeting of cultures, seeing the similarities and differences between religions and even between local versions of myths. So educated people in the Hellenistic world were used to hearing or reading differing versions of the standard myths of the pagan gods and concluded that these stories were not entirely true in their literal sense.

Even though myth remained a living force, and though the pagan world (and arguably the Jewish world too) continued to be familiar with myth, by the first and second centuries CE it was not considered a primary vehicle for religious thought. Plato had written his own beautiful myths, such as the myth of Er, to illustrate his philosophy, yet he banned myth, along with poetry, from his ideal republic, despite his own facility with both forms, and philosophy had won over as the primary mode of spiritual expression for the Hellenistic world. In fact, there is nothing similar to the Gnostic use of myth at that time. The mystery religions had their own myths, but the creative use of myth in Gnosticism was unique.

Most ancient Gnostics probably had some sense of their myths not being literally true, because they were eager to adapt and alter those myths. Gnostic mythopoeia (the creation of myths) was dynamic not static. Yet we can never quite see things through the eyes of ancient Gnostics, and it is better for us to view the Gnostic myths as spiritual metaphor allegory. If anyone in the twenty-first century were to view these myths too literally, we should surely suspect paranoia.

In the Gnostic mythos, the fall has affected both individual humans and the entire cosmos. It was a fall from the spiritual realm into the material world – the cosmos – which itself came into existence only because of the fall. There was no earthly paradise at the beginning of time, no garden full of flowers and fruit in which Adam and Eve walked contentedly until they ate the fruit of the wrong tree (which in some Gnostic interpretations was the right tree – the tree of knowledge is the tree of *gnosis*). There was no Golden Age for mankind. What was created was not a garden but a prison, and the creator was not the omnipotent, wise, all-loving God, but an ignorant, half-mad craftsman who was himself the result of a fall. Yet the fall was not committed by man, and was not a punishment for disobedience, so mankind is not cursed with the burden of original sin, but is merely asleep to its true nature.

Inasmuch as Gnostics may have looked to a Golden Age, they found it still existing, eternal, in the spiritual realm of the Pleroma. There are very many accounts of the formation of the Pleroma, the realm of fullness. According to some, the diversity of the various divine beings that populate the Pleroma ('fullness') began when God contemplated himself. God saw himself, as in a mirror or as in water, and in viewing his image emanated aeons, versions of himself which each express some quality of the One. The aeons constitute the Pleroma, the fullness and completeness and perfection of the one God. The concept of aeons and the Pleroma can be confusing at first, not least because of the unfamiliarity of terms.

We might consider the aeons from a variety of viewpoints: they are mythological entities, and when we are considering myth it is perhaps best to view them as personages. However, many of them are named after psychological attributes or abstract qualities, many of which are inner qualities. We might translate the aeons as 'eternals', that is, as beings or qualities that exist in eternity, or as hypostases, qualities of God.

We have already seen that according to Gnostic myth the youngest aeon, Sophia, fell from the Pleroma due either to her curiosity or dissatisfaction and gave birth to the demiurge. The demiurge is the creator God – the God who crafted this world – but is distinct from the absolute deity. The concept of the demiurge first appeared in Plato's *Timaeus*, where the word simply means 'craftsman', 'artisan' or also a person in authority. Plato's demiurge was the good creator of the world, who made the world good, but it was the young gods that made the human being, and so some imperfections were involved in the creation of humanity.

Plato did not set out a rigorous cosmological system, and in other dialogues he has seemingly contradictory views on what is the highest power in the world. It is perhaps as a result of trying to reconcile the concepts of the good, the pre-existent forms and the demiurge – all fundamental aspects of Platonic thought – that the idea of the demiurge as a lower, inferior God came about. In any case, the Gnostics adapted Platonic ideas to their own ends, and their treatment of the demiurge, who in the hands of Gnostics has become an ignorant, inferior creator, is almost as revolutionary an interpretation of Platonism as it is of the Bible.

The word 'illegitimate' is perhaps a good description of the Gnostic demiurge. He is sometimes described as an abortion, and he often has no father, or his father is darkness or nothingness or matter or some lower element. But his creation is also illegitimate in the sense of being wrong, or not appropriate. The demiurge filled the world with archons, the rulers, ghastly counterparts of the spiritual aeons. The archons tended to have strange barbarous names that did not have a clear meaning in any language, or alternatively were like parodies of the aeons, expressing qualities of the psyche that is trapped in materiality. The word 'archon' may be translated as 'authority', 'ruler', 'governor'. The archons are the malicious minions of the demiurge. Sometimes they have a particular role in creating the human body, and, psychologically, the multiplicity of the archons reflects the multiplicity of human thoughts, turning this way and that, distracted by myriad influences of external life and the physical world.

* * *

It is time now to look at some specific Gnostic myths. While the ideas of the Gnostics may be immediately stimulating and recognizable to modern minds, the ancient texts containing Gnostic cosmogonies and other myths can often appear dry in summary and bewildering when read from the sources. The authors of these source texts did not have tidy minds. They embroidered and interpolated and rewrote earlier texts, and the end results are often somewhat confusing. Throughout my retellings of the myths I will interject and interpret, and the reader should remember that these are interpretations. Some of them are mine; many represent the standard understandings of scholarship. The reader should eventually wish to read the original texts in one of the more readable translations.[1]

The story of Adam and Eve, which takes up a mere couple of chapters in Genesis, has always been fertile ground for religious interpretation and exposition. The brief account is full of mysterious details and contradictions. Mankind is created male and female, 'So God created man in his own image, in the image of God created he him; male and female created he them,' states Genesis 1:27, yet in 2:21–4, 'And the Lord God caused a deep sleep to fall upon Adam, and he slept: and he took one of his ribs, and closed up the flesh instead thereof; And the rib, which the Lord God had taken from man, made he a woman, and brought her unto the man'. The male is created first and the female is created from the male. Which of these versions is correct? The Gnostics answered that Adam and Eve represent different parts of a human being, and harmonize the accounts by viewing them in this way.

Judaism, Christianity and Islam proudly proclaim that they are monotheistic religions, worshipping a single God who created the world, yet in Genesis 3: 22, God contemplates that 'the man has become like one of us'. Why is God referring to himself in the plural, and why are there two creations of mankind? Rabbinical and Christian interpreters have also glossed and allegorized these passages in order to make a consistent sense of them. The Gnostics answered that the plural 'us' refers to the many archons that serve the demiurge, and in the light of this they made the archons the creators and rulers of the human body.

The scholarly explanation for these two creations is that the book of Genesis (and all five books of the Torah or Pentateuch) combined elements from older accounts. This explanation is known as the Documentary Hypothesis. Thus the Book of Genesis, far from being the earliest religious scripture of the Jewish people, was compiled in the fifth century BCE, and was a patchwork of much older material. Chapter 1 of Genesis is identified as being derived from a document labelled by scholars 'P' for Priestly source, because of its ecclesiastical interests and the likelihood of it having been written by sixth-century BCE priests of Israel, the northern territory of the Hebrews, whereas most of chapter 2, including the creation of woman from the side of man, is part of the 'J' source: 'J' for Jahwist or Yahwist, the name of God, which is traditionally rendered into English as Jehovah. Thus, according to the scholarly analysis, the two creations of man are simply the result of trying to harmonize conflicting traditions.

The Documentary Hypothesis is well considered among modern scholars, but was unknown to the ancients, who in any case were concerned with the meaning of their scriptures, not the textual history. Jewish scholars studied the Hebrew Bible (or its Greek translation, the Septuagint) in minute detail and argued back and forth the meaning of each sentence and phrase. In turn, Genesis was discussed not only in a purely Jewish rabbinical setting, but also in a Platonic context – as in the writings of Philo of Alexandria, who allegorized Adam and Eve in a proto-Gnostic way as mind and sensation respectively – in some Hellenistic Christian writings, and in the writings of the Gnostics. In the usual Christian or Jewish interpretations, the tale of Adam and Eve, the serpent (who was not explicitly identified with Satan until the first century) and the Garden of Eden is a story of sin, of a fall from grace, of temptation and defeat, of disobedience and punishment.

If the Jewish law came from Moses as a revelation from the Jewish God, and the Jewish people follow these teachings, yet the Jewish God still allows the Romans to rule Judea, destroy the Temple and exile the Jewish people from Judea, then from these events what can be concluded of the Jewish God and his teachings? And likewise, if Christians practise their faith and yet are oppressed and persecuted, ridiculed and forced into martyrdom, what does that say of the Christian God?

Some Jews, particularly those of the rabbinical-pharisaical movement, would say that the Temple was destroyed because they had not kept the Torah as strictly as God had wished. Some Christians would say that martyrdom was a holy act of overwhelming faith in Christ which would be rewarded with everlasting life. Gnostics looked at the ruins of the Jewish Temple, at the dispersion and exile of the Jews, at the growing literalness of Christian worship and the stubbornness of

Christians rushing headlong into death, and concluded that the failure was not merely in the worshippers, but in the nature of the God that they served.

If, as the Platonists stated, this world was created by a demiurge, and if, as the experience of many people suggested, this world is a corrupt world, full of pain, a dense and ignorant world, then surely the account of the creation in Genesis is the story of an ignorant God creating the physical, suffering human body. Had this God known otherwise, and had he the best intentions for humankind, surely he would have focused on the world of the spirit instead, and thus the creator God must be either unaware of the spiritual world or a malign and cruel God. So the Gnostics were particularly concerned with cosmogony, the creation of the world, and anthropogony, the creation of man, because something had clearly gone wrong in both cases. How else could the wars that ravaged the first and second centuries be explained?

A number of surviving Gnostic texts have addressed this in their idiosyncratic ways. In the Sethian Gnostic text, *The Hypostasis of the Archons* (or, *The Reality of the Rulers*, the extreme difference between the renderings of this title being an indication of the difficulties involved in translating Coptic Gnostic texts), Ialdabaoth (better pronounced Yal-da-ba-oth than Yal-Day-bay-oth or Yal-dah-bay-oth) is the blind and ignorant leader of the archons. A voice that comes from 'incorruptibility' (the Pleroma) identifies him as Samael, 'God of the blind'. His identity as the Hebrew God is left in no doubt when he asserts 'It is I who am God; there is none apart from me'.[2]

The archons fashioned a human being after the image of the aeon named Incorruptibility, whose reflection they had seen when

Incorruptibility gazed into the waters. This is probably an interpretation of the darkness moving on the face of the waters in Genesis 1:2. In *The Hypostasis of the Archons*, it is the archons who create Adam's physical body and Ialdabaoth, in the role of the Hebrew God, who breathes life into Adam's face. Adam accordingly comes to life but is unable to rise from the ground. Symbolically, he cannot raise himself up from matter because what Ialdabaoth has given him is not spirit, but soul, a lower level of existence that is associated with the demiurge in many Gnostic systems. Soul is the quintessential human element, poised between the material and the divine, between the body and the spirit.

The demiurge and archons kept blowing 'like storm winds' but they could not make the modelled form (Adam) resemble the image of Incorruptibility that they had seen in the waters. Thus the human creation was faulty from the start. But the aeon Spirit from the Adamantine realm, that is, the Pleroma again, saw Adam and descended into him. Thus a spiritual element entered into humanity despite the efforts of the demiurge and the archons.

Incorruptibility then called for assistance for Adam, and for an unstated reason it was the archons who actually listened to Incorruptibility and created the familiar setting of the Garden of Eden as a home for Adam. It was the ignorant archons who told Adam that he could eat of any tree except the tree of gnosis of good and evil, but – and this is an important twist – the archons were acting unwittingly according to the instructions of Incorruptibility and it was by this ruse that Spirit was able to affect humanity. We can see that this is all an interpretation of Genesis 1, and the causes of the events are taken away from God and appropriately but unsystematically distributed among and attributed to Ialdabaoth, his archons, or to the aeon Incorruptibility, who plays a role resembling a true God.

This retelling of the creation of man turns the traditional meaning on its head, but it also clarifies the purpose of the creation and fall. Adam does not fall from Paradise, but escapes the clutches of Ialdabaoth and his archons. Even in creating man, the demiurge and the archons are unable to stop the influence of the spiritual realm.

The archons, being the rulers of the material world, put Adam into a deep sleep, which is identified with ignorance or the lack of gnosis. They opened up his side and inserted flesh in place of the living woman that they found there, and this is probably intended as further symbolism of spirit and soul, where the woman represents the spirit that is taken away by the archons, so that Adam is once again 'merely animate', possessing body and soul, but being without spirit. In *The Hypostasis* the female element therefore represents the spirit and is therefore higher than the male, who may stand for the soul. The archons have caused the spirit to be separated from the body of Adam, which was created by the archons, and the soul of Adam, breathed in by Ialdabaoth.

When Adam meets the spirit-endowed woman Eve, who is both part of him and yet from a higher realm, he recognizes that she is the source of his life and he calls her the mother of the living. She is both mother and midwife. But the archons are also attracted to the woman and attempt to rape her, and in order to escape she turns into a tree – possibly a reference to the two trees of Paradise, but also reminiscent of the myth of Daphne.

The spirit, the feminine principle, then escapes from the

spirit-endowed woman into the serpent, leaving Eve vacant of spirit! So now we have both Adam and Eve consisting of body and soul with no spirit, Adam's spirit having been extracted into Eve, and Eve's spirit having escaped into the serpent. The snake debates with the woman, persuading her to eat of the forbidden fruit, and then the spirit leaves the snake. When the carnal Adam and Eve eat of the tree, their ignorance, or lack of gnosis, is revealed to them. They are naked of the spiritual element, gnosis.

But the chief archon comes to Adam and Eve, as does God in the Genesis account, and asks the same questions of them concerning their nakedness and shame as the Jewish God asked. In *The Hypostasis*, these questions are addressed only to the carnal parts because their spiritual element has slithered away.

Subsequently Adam and Eve are thrown into the distraction of life. They give birth to Cain and Abel, the first murderer and first victim, but then to their third son, Seth, who is considered as an important third principle, the quintessential Gnostic, not subject to the calamity that overcame Cain and Abel, and then to Norea, a female figure who is in many ways similar to Seth. In *The Hypostasis*, Norea is the virgin that the archons did not defile, a woman who was not subject to the influence of the archons, and the future of humanity thus depends on Norea and the angel Eleleth who aids her.

Obviously, this account is not entirely consistent in its symbolism or in the way that it reinterprets Genesis. It has become its own myth and is capable of additional elaboration, explanation and interpretation. It is largely a psychological or pneumatalogical myth, a myth concerned with the origin and importance of the soul and the spirit in contrast to the evil of the material world. For the Gnostics, cosmology was inseparable from psychology.

Man is therefore created via two principles — his soul and body from the demiurge and archons, and his spirit from Incorruptibility and the Pleroma. The lower principles, the archons, are unwittingly influenced by the higher. Adam, Eve and the serpent are seen as successive hosts for the spirit. It remains for Norea to host the spirit and fulfil her destiny, and she will not be controlled by Ialdabaoth or the archons. Thus the creation of man is an attempt by the world rulers to imitate a higher power, yet by this ruse the archons create a model by which the spirit may enter into man as an element that is beyond the worldly creation.

The Revelation of Adam, or *Apocalypse of Adam*, is purportedly a teaching given by Adam to Seth, his third son. In this version of the myth, once Adam and Eve have been created, Eve, being the higher aspect of the couple, teaches Adam about the gnosis of the eternal God, and the two of them live in glory like angels. But the lower God, the God of the archons, despising their union, angrily commands them to separate from each other, and they become as humans are now and know and worship the lower God instead of the true God. Their hearts become darkened. Yet Adam perceives three figures which come from the higher God, and which the lower God cannot see, and these urge him to arise from the sleep of death. But the creator God incites Adam and Eve to procreate and their indulgence in sex means that they are thus lost to gnosis.

They indulge in external copulation instead of the internal union of the bridal chamber, and become the parents of mankind in the created world instead of maintaining their gnosis of the true God. Redemption must be left for later, and it comes through the race of Seth, those who wish for gnosis, and the saviour who brings revelation to humanity.

In *The Apocryphon of John*, John the son of Zebedee is harangued by a Pharisee named Arimanios. The Pharisee taunts John with the question 'Where is your teacher?' knowing full well that, according to the gospel story, his teacher, Jesus, has been crucified. John replies instead that Jesus has returned to the place that he came from. As John contemplates the reason for the saviour's arrival in this world and his departure from it, he sees a great light illuminating all of creation and a human form that changes in turn from a child to an old man to a young man. The man begins to teach John and launches into a classic description of the Sethian Gnostic myth. The lesson is clear: the departure of the saviour (the title used throughout the *Apocryphon of John*) by crucifixion has in no way cut John off from the truth, or from the saviour himself. Many of the Gnostic dialogues between Jesus and his disciples are post-resurrection, emphasizing that it is not one's earthly contact with Jesus that is important, but one's own direct relationship to the light.

In the *Gospel of Judas* Jesus recounts to Judas a similar version of the Sethian Gnostic myth. He teaches Judas separately from the other disciples, before he goes knowingly to his death. The irrelevance of the crucifixion is a common factor in many Gnostic texts. In the canonical gospels, the crucifixion is the centre and focus of the story, the actions and teachings of Jesus foreshadowing the great event of the crucifixion, which is the highlight not only of the life of Jesus, but of human history in general. Yet in Gnostic accounts, the crucifixion is almost incidental. If Jesus were principally a spirit, how could the murder of his physical body make any difference to his spiritual essence? If it is gnosis that provides salvation, not Christ's atoning death, then it is the secret teachings of Jesus, concerned with our own illumination and an understanding of our place in the universe and the human predicament, that are important, not the expiration of a corpse in a Roman execution. In other versions of the myth, Seth, not Jesus, is the redeemer figure, and in Manichaeism it is Mani, who follows on in a long line of revealers stretching back to Adam.

So this is the situation that we are in. We were created by the ignorant rulers of this world, who continue to influence us, but the divine beings of the higher realms have seen fit to allow us to partake of spirit. The influence of the archons means that the history of humanity is a history of internecine warfare, of petty squabbles caused by ignorance of the true spiritual realm. But redeemers like Seth and Jesus have come down to us and revealed to us the true state of the world. If we accept the knowledge that they bring, we can directly know the spiritual world and God, and can rise up from the sleep in which we live, the ignorance in which we flounder.

Saviours or redeemers have come from the Pleroma to bring knowledge and Gnostic teaching to the world. But the followers of these teachers eventually misunderstood or perverted the teachings, or lapsed into the degraded religious forms that the archons have promoted and thus understood Ialdabaoth to be the true God. Teachings that were originally intended to show mankind its position in the universe and to offer some guidance towards knowledge of God, and hence escape from the prison of this world, instead keep us in prison. And so organized religion keeps mankind asleep and, intentionally or unintentionally, upholds the illusory view of the world promoted by the demiurge and his archons.

In the *Gospel of Judas* the disciples (and perhaps even Judas) continue to worship and sacrifice to the false God despite the presence of Jesus in the world. Conventional religion worships the wrong God, the God of this world, rather than the true God who is unknown and yet can be known by gnosis.

CHAPTER 2

SETHIANS, VALENTINANS AND OTHERS

On first encountering the Gnostics, the modern reader will tend to assume that they were a unified group of people, an ancient Christian movement in competition with orthodox Catholic Christianity. The writings of Christian heresiologists such as Irenaeus might give quite the opposite impression, that there were dozens of competing Gnostic groups with strange and obscure names – Barbelites, Barbelognostics, Cainites, Ophites, Naasenes, Cerdonians, Borborians and many others.

Since the discovery of the Nag Hammadi Library and the decades of research and analysis that followed, modern historians have tended to divide the ancient Gnostics proper into two groupings: the Sethians and the Valentinians. There were certainly many other heretical groups (Epiphanius catalogues 80 heresies of various types, some of which have no relationship to Christianity), and there were important forms of Christianity that had Gnostic connections, without being wholly Gnostic, such as the Syrian Thomasine Christians who appealed to the figure of St Thomas, or the dualist Marcionites, but most of the ancient Gnostic literature can be divided along the lines of Sethianism or Valentinianism.

The Gnostics in general lived ordinary lives – they were not monks or nuns, did not live apart in closeted religious communities; they were 'in this world but not of it'. Broadly speaking, the Valentinians were able to integrate themselves into the proto-orthodox Christian Church, whereas the Sethians were a quite separate movement, though they did consider themselves to be Christians. For the greater part of their history, the Valentinians saw themselves more as the esoteric side of the mainstream Christian Church, even if the leaders of that Church were not inclined to reciprocate. Sethian organization was perhaps more akin to that of the Hellenistic mystery religions. Sethians were members of a closed society that considered its members to be the seed of Seth, the third son of Adam and Eve, and they were the portion of humanity that had received gnosis and could thus have a different fate to the rest of mankind who followed the pattern of Cain and Abel, murderer and victim. And it was the Sethians who were most clearly labelled as Gnostic in the works of the heresiologists.

Sethian thought is represented in the 2006 Kasser et al *Gospel of Judas*, as well as in the following works from the Nag Hammadi Library: *The Apocalypse of Adam*, *The Hypostasis of the Archons*, *The Three Steles of Seth*, *Allogenes* and, crucially, *The Apocryphon of John*. The last in this list is the best attested of any Gnostic texts, being preserved in three of the Nag Hammadi codices and in the Berlin Gnostic codex. It is one of the most complete expressions of the Gnostic myth and, at least according to our surviving manuscripts, the most popular Gnostic text.

Seth was also an important figure in heterodox Jewish literature around the same period, and his life story and significance is amplified and expanded in Jewish apocryphal and rabbinical literature. Sethian texts contain phrases such as 'the seed of Seth', or 'the children of Seth', or the 'race' or 'generation' of Seth. The Sethians also referred to themselves as 'the immovable race' or 'unshakeable race', possibly meaning that, whatever the other vagaries of history, Gnostics always existed. Alternatively they could have been contrasting the imperishability and stability of the spiritual realm, the Pleroma, with the material world. The scholar Bentley Layton coined the term 'classical Gnosticism' to refer to the Sethians and they are in many ways the most typical Gnostic movement.

Sethian mythology is notable for the female mother figure of Barbelo, who is the first emanation of the father God. The name Barbelo may have come from Hebrew originally and may have meant 'God in four'. Such is Barbelo's importance to the Sethian mythology that Sethians were often referred to as Barbeloites or Barbelognostics. The Sethians often made reference to a trinity of divine beings: a family of father, mother and son. The mother is Barbelo, the son is called Autogenes, the self-generated, or, as in other Gnostic systems, he is sometimes the Anthropos, the archetypal human. Four angels illuminate the Autogenes – Harmozel, Oroiael, Daueithai and Eleleth. The demiurge is named Yaldabaoth, Saklas or Nebruel and is usually identified with the Jewish God.

The Sethians held baptisms and their sacraments were known

as the five seals. John Turner, an academic who is the leading expert on the Sethians, has suggested that they, like the Mandaeans, may have originated as a baptismal sect along the lines of John the Baptist's disciples, or the Essenes. In the Dead Sea Scrolls we see evidence of a Jewish sect (possibly but not necessarily the Essenes) with dualistic qualities (dark versus light) that withdrew its support from the central Jerusalem Temple. It is possible that the inversionary element of Sethianism originates from a similar process of Jews who rejected the centralized Jewish faith, but went a step further in a radical rejection of conventional Judaism and saw the mainstream Jewish religion as a tool of the demiurge. Be that as it may, there are strong Jewish elements in Sethianism.

John Turner has proposed a complex development of Sethian Gnosticism based on the literary history of the surviving texts and their layers of development. According to Turner, Sethianism may have originated as a 'non-Christian baptismal sect of the first centuries BCE and CE'.[3] These early Sethians would have seen Adam and Seth as divine revealer figures and looked forward to an apocalyptic return of Seth in the near future. *The Apocalypse of Adam*, a Sethian text in the Nag Hammadi Library, which may date to the mid-second century or even earlier, has no definite Christian features. In a second stage of development, Seth may have been identified with Christ (as is stated in some NHL texts) in the early decades of Christianity as Christian and Sethian groups came into contact with each other.

Thus the Sethians developed into a form of Christian Gnosticism and attached themselves to the quite variegated Christian movements of the time, and it is at this time that they were attacked by Irenaeus. But as the proto-orthodox Church became more powerful, heterodox groups like the Sethians were forced out, and the Sethians themselves may have rejected the Christian elements in their systems. Turner sees a further stage in which the Sethians, having been estranged from the community of mainstream Christianity, then turned towards a more Platonic emphasis, and identified themselves with the classical philosophical current, which eventually led to them being rejected once again by mainstream Platonists such as the Neoplatonist Plotinus. Turner proposes that this further rejection led to a fragmentation of Sethianism into various groups such as the Audians, Borborites, Archontics and Phibionites, some of which survived into the early Middle Ages.

This conjectural history is not incompatible with the notion that the Sethians originated in Egypt, which had a large Jewish population and its own temple. In one of those suggestive muddles of history, Seth/Set was an Egyptian God too, who was sometimes associated with the Jewish people.[4]

The Archontics, one of the successor groups to the Sethians, are given an interesting history by the fourth-century heresy hunter Epiphanius, who located them from the middle of the fourth century in Armenia. According to Epiphanius, an Armenian named Eutaktus was returning from Egypt (a hotbed of Gnosticism of course) and stopped off in Palestine, where he was introduced to Peter the Gnostic, a cave-dwelling hermit who lived an isolated existence relieved only by his pupils who visited him in his cave. Peter had been a Christian priest but was expelled from the priesthood for heresy. Epiphanius connects Peter's Gnostic conversion with time spent in Arabia, possibly with Ebionites and Nazoreans, neither of which groups were Gnostic per se but were Jewish-Christian sects with strong ascetic or encratite leanings. When Eutaktus returned to Armenia, he taught Peter's Gnostic doctrine to his pupils, who included a senator and other rich, high-ranking people, so he must have had considerable influence in Armenian high society. The descriptions of the teachings of the Archontics given by Epiphanius (collected in two lost books, the *Lesser Harmony* and *Greater Harmony*) show that they were very Sethian.

* * *

No orthodox Christian mystic could approve of the inversionary tactics of the Sethians. No desert father or orthodox monk writing in the *Philokalia*, no illuminated Catholic saint could approve of the denigration of Moses, or the elevation of the serpent, or the dismissal of the Mosaic God as the ignorant demiurge. But the other great branch of Gnosticism, the Valentinian, found a way of coming to terms with proto-orthodox Christianity and of adapting itself to ecclesiastical forms so that it could provide an inner meaning to complement external Christianity.

The tale of the Gnostics is not a story of grand individuals, realized masters surrounded by their student minions, but of many, many sincere Gnostics, most of whom were not set down in recorded history and so are now anonymous. Their saviours and revealers, Adam, Seth, Norea, even Jesus, were not seen as historical characters or recent teachers but mythical figures existing in mythical time. Most of the individual Gnostics, great and small, are lost to history, and even those whose names we know are not well represented historically. Valentinus was certainly not the earliest Gnostic, but he might easily be considered the most brilliant and the most influential. Since the time of Irenaeus it has been asserted that Valentinus adapted

existing Gnostic teaching to his own system, further
Christianizing it and removing or de-emphasizing some of the
elements that clashed too much with other Christian theologies.

Despite his relative fame, the details we have of Valentinus
are sketchy. Valentinus was born and grew up in Egypt in the
Nile Delta around the beginning of the second century. The
elegance of his writing and the beauty of his metaphors indicate
that he had probably emerged from a fine education in rhetoric
and philosophy. His writings survive only in small fragments
quoted by Church Fathers such as Clement of Alexandria, and
in the beautiful and profound Nag Hammadi treatise the *Gospel
of Truth*, which has been attributed to Valentinus with some
confidence – Irenaeus refers to it as the gospel of the
Valentinians. The *Gospel of Truth* is a poetic sermon that
instructs the Gnostic to awaken and cast off ignorance.

Valentinus was claimed to have a spiritual lineage that went
back to St Paul. It was said that he had been taught by the
otherwise unknown Theudas, who had himself been a disciple
of Paul. The writings of Paul, 'the great apostle', have many Gnostic
features and were a strong influence in Valentinian Gnosticism.
Whether Valentinus might have received his Gnostic doctrine
from Theudas or whether this merely gave him a claim to
apostolic succession that was essential in his efforts to influence
the mainstream Church is unclear. It is also possible that
Valentinus may have known Basilides, a slightly earlier Gnostic
or proto-Gnostic teacher who was in Alexandria around the
same time as him. From Alexandria, Valentinus went to Rome
in the late 130s where he became involved with the mainstream
Roman Church. Valentinus rose so high in the Roman Christian
Church that it is said that he stood for the post of Bishop of Rome,

but he was unsuccessful in the election and left Rome shortly after this.

The teaching of Valentinus and of subsequent Valentinians has two sides to it, which are sometimes difficult to reconcile. One side of Valentinus' teaching relied heavily on a technique of elegant allegorical interpretation that had its roots in the Alexandrian tradition. There are some remarkable similarities between Philo's platonizing interpretation of the biblical Torah and Valentinus' approach to scripture. Texts like the *Gospel of Philip*, which is an anthology that contains a good sample of Valentinian interpretation and interests (though it is not by Valentinus himself), or the *Gospel of Truth* are full of metaphor and esoteric interpretation. They are among the most accessible of the Nag Hammadi tractates. But also there is a vast Valentinian cosmology, which survives mainly in the reports of the Church Fathers and which has strong similarities with other Gnostic systems.

The Valentinians' own allegorical interpretations adapted extracts from the gospels and Paul to the cosmological system. The simpler Valentinian allegorization, which is often to do with the interrelationship of body, soul and spirit, is generally more convincing than the cosmological interpretation. (See the next chapter for more on the Gnostic interpretation of scripture.)

Even though they traced themselves back to Valentinus as a revered teacher, and accepted Church hierarchy when they came into contact with it, the Valentinians were notoriously democratic and egalitarian in their dealings with each other. The Church Father Tertullian complained that he could see no strict hierarchy among them, 'First, one does not know which is a catchumen or a believer. They enter on equal terms, they listen on equal terms, they pray on equal terms... they do not care if they confess different doctrines, provided that they all help to destroy the truth... And so today, one man is a bishop, tomorrow another. Today one is a deacon who tomorrow will be a lector. The presbyter of today is the layman of tomorrow. Even the members of the laity are charged with the duties of a priest.'[5]

The Church Father Irenaeus also had first-hand experience of Valentinians. Irenaeus became Bishop of Lugdunum in Gaul (modern Lyon in France). He was dismayed to find that there were many Valentinians in his diocese, and, being particularly concerned that he couldn't easily tell them apart from other Christians, he described them as the usual wolves in sheep's clothing. Irenaeus insisted that Valentinus' lineage went to Simon Magus rather than Paul.

The Valentinians accepted as scripture the writings that became part of the emerging Christian canon, but interpreted them esoterically. Texts such as the *Gospel of Truth*, the *Gospel of Philip*, the *Letter to Flora* and the *Treatise on the Resurrection* make subtle use of the imagery of Christianity but press it into the service of spiritual metaphor.

The Sethians, in contrast, wrote sprawling epics that reinterpreted the Bible, reinterpreted Platonism and finally reinterpreted their own interpretations. The creation of the spiritual universe, the identity of the demiurge, the saviour figures of Seth and Norea, the pre- and post-deluge history of mankind were worked over in endless attempts at theme and variation.

By the latter part of the second century and the beginning of the third, Valentinians had spread out through the Roman Empire. They considered themselves part of the universal Catholic Church, attended Mass, valued sacraments and partook of most of the conventional Christian moralities and practices. But they also had their own rites and they held separate meetings at which they discussed (and presumably practised) the inner meanings of the scriptures. Like their founder Valentinus, the Valentinians were well educated and their allegorical techniques were philosophically intelligent. Their interpretative methods had their influence on Clement of Alexandria and Origen, the allegorizing Alexandrian Church Fathers who, although they refuted Gnostic doctrine, were sympathetic to many of its points of emphasis and its allegorical techniques.

The Valentinians divided humanity into three groups: the hylic, or choic, who were aligned with matter or the body; the psychic, who were identified with the soul; and the pneumatic, who were spiritual. At their most esoteric, these categories were surely related to one's current experience, not to hard-and-fast categories of human potential and 'election' – whether one's inner world could currently be categorized as concerned mainly with matter or with the soul (for instance, human emotions and human culture) or with the spirit. But for some Valentinians these seem to have become fixed categories and connected with pre-election. So, the Valentinians themselves were pneumatic, ordinary Christians were psychic and pagans were hylic. The Gnostics were not free of what might politely be called group dynamics, and apostates, those Valentinians who left the sect, did not have a good fate awaiting them. Yet on the whole, the Valentinians were the most reasonable and adaptable of the Gnostics.

* * *

Aside from the Sethians and Valentians, one more Gnostic-related movement must be mentioned here: Marcionism, named after the second-century religious leader Marcion of Pontus. Only the bare outlines of Marcion's life are known to us. Marcion was born around the end of the first century in Sinope near the Black Sea in Asia Minor. It is likely that he grew up in a Christian community, perhaps one that particularly valued the writings of Paul or had a connection to Paul's missionizing (traditionally the 'seven churches of Asia Minor' were Ephesus, Smyrna, Pergamum, Thyatira, Sardis, Philadelphia, Laodikea), and his father may have been a bishop in addition to his profession as a wealthy shipowner.

According to the Church Father Irenaeus, Marcion was taught by the Syrian Gnostic Cerdo, whom he may have first met in Rome in the 140s. Irenaeus also tells us that Cerdo derived his teaching from the followers of Simon Magus, and he taught that the God of the Hebrews was not the God of Jesus. The old God and his works were all too familiar, the new one was unknown, the old God was merely righteous, but the new one truly good. This last point is an important one. In the systems of Cerdo and Marcion, the Old Testament God is not always considered evil, or even ignorant, but he is a God of righteousness and law, not of mercy and salvation, a view with which many modern Christians could agree. Yet, as Irenaeus says, the Old Testament God is declared by Marcion 'to be the author of evils, to take delight in war, to be infirm of purpose, and even to be contrary to Himself.'[6]

Marcionism is dualistic and Gnostic-influenced, but not truly Gnostic because it left out the single most crucial element of Gnosticism: gnosis. As is usual, we know of Marcion's doctrine chiefly through the heresiologists, and they dispute not with Marcion himself but with his successors and with the Church that he founded. Like Mani after him, Marcion founded a distinct religion, and in Marcion's case it was a form of Christianity that became a major competitor to Catholic Christianity.

Marcion rejected the gospels of Matthew, Mark, John and all of the apocryphal gospels, and used only the Gospel of Luke, and a cut-down version of Luke at that, which, according to Irenaeus, had been stripped of any material that might contradict Marcion's own doctrine. The epistles of Paul were also part of his canon, in distinctly Marcionite recensions, and Irenaeus accused Marcion of 'dismembering' those too. Other letters, like those attributed to Peter or John, were excluded from Marcion's canon.

The influence of Paul's writings in Marcionism is as clear as it is in Valentinianism. New Testament scholars have seen Marcion as a predecessor of textual criticism, the discipline that applies logical, critical reasoning to the differing versions of ancient texts in order to re-establish the original form. Marcion decided that sections of Luke and the epistles contained interpolations that had been added by Christians who were trying to push Christianity back in the direction of Judaism, back to worshipping the God of the Mosaic law. Of course, Marcion's textual criticism was anything but neutral, and in reality he was simply expunging the text of elements that did not support his position.

Ten Pauline epistles (I and II Corinthians, Romans, I and II Thessalonians, Ephesians, Colossians, Philemon, Philippians and Galatians, the last of which he considered the most fundamental statement of doctrine) were approved by Marcion, and he agrees with modern scholarship in rejecting the Pastoral Epistles (Titus and the two letters to Timothy) as not being authentically Pauline. The Dutch radical view, now supported by Robert Price, argues that Marcion in fact wrote the Pauline epistles himself because we do not find references to Paul's letters before the time of Marcion, and they are first quoted in quantity by the Church Fathers in opposition to Marcion's mangling of them.

Of course, we do not have any autograph manuscripts, and there may well have been a great deal of variation and interpolation in the transmission of the gospels and the epistles before our earliest surviving copies and fragments. But this kind of radical criticism leaves us without any firm ground or fixed point with which to reconstruct history and is probably just an artefact of the accidental survival of the literature. Marcion's insistence on the Gospel of Luke and the Pauline letters amounted to an attempt to establish the first Christian canon, and the subsequent efforts by Catholic Church leaders to define their own canon were initiated in reaction to Marcion's. Thus he was indirectly responsible for the compilation of the New Testament as an official collection of Christian scripture.

Marcion believed that Jesus descended into Hades after death and that he freed the souls that he found there. He uses this as a tool by which the Old Testament assessment of important Bible figures can be inverted, in a typically Gnostic way. Cain, the Sodomites, the Egyptians, and other nations that had been enemies of the Hebrews were saved by Jesus, according to Marcion, while Abel, Enoch, Noah and the prophets were not.

Marcion became part of a Christian community in Rome. His background in shipping had made him wealthy and he is credited as having donated a large sum to the Roman Church, which was returned to him when he was expelled for his heterodox beliefs in 144 CE. We do not know much of Marcion's subsequent life, but he was successful in establishing a Church that thrived in the East and West for a couple of centuries. In the

West it was vanquished in the fourth century by the anti-heretical laws passed by the Christian Roman emperors, while in the East it limped on until the fifth or sixth centuries, perhaps surviving in small pockets for considerably longer, and in other places being absorbed by Manichaeism.

Marcion's teaching was dualistic but lacked the developed mythology of truly Gnostic systems. In particular, there was no explanation of how the world came to be as it is. The Old Testament was rejected, and with it the Book of Genesis, and any real cosmogony was lost. We are left with the bare facts that the Old Testament God of law is opposed to the Christian God of salvation, but we are not given any original cosmic reason for this opposition, which is something the great Gnostic systems of Sethianism and Valentinianism do so well.

A generation later, a pupil of Marcion named Apelles adapted Marcion's system to bring it more into line with other Gnostic teachings, and he included cosmogonical myths. Although his doctrines were Gnostic in their origin, Marcion was not a Gnostic because his teachings lacked the key element of gnosis itself, and as a result, the Marcionites tended towards dogma. Marcionism was a direct competitor to Catholic Christianity, and a successful one at that.

Most Gnostics did not agree with the Jewish or Christian view of the Old Testament, but they wrestled with it. They inverted the meaning of stories, they turned the story of Adam and Eve in Eden into a single episode of another grand myth, which they allegorized and interpreted. Female characters represented the soul, as did Israel, as did the Beloved in the Song of Songs. God was the ignorant demiurge, Seth and Noah were archetypal Gnostics, but Moses was merely a mouthpiece for the demiurge. Marcion's attitude to the Old Testament, on the other hand, represented a narrowing down, and a restrictive approach: he simply outlawed it, excluded it from his Bible just as he excluded Mark, Matthew and John (and as those responsible for the developmentary process of the standard Western Christian Bible canon effectively excluded the *Gospel of Thomas* and any Gnostic texts from their compilation).

Marcionism is Gnosticism Lite, Gnosticism without the gnosis, an adaptation of Gnostic ideas to orthodox Christianity that could satisfy neither Gnostic nor Catholic. But despite its derivative nature, Marcionism captured the popular imagination in a way that Gnosticism proper could not, rather like a second-century Dan Brown. Paradoxically, it may be the lack of gnosis in Marcion's teaching that made it successful. If his Church had appeared a little earlier it might easily have supplanted the Catholic Church as the most popular version of Christianity. But still it would not have been truly Gnostic.

CHAPTER 3

AS ABOVE SO BELOW: GNOSTIC PSYCHOLOGY

'Once the soul had wings,
but the soul lost her wings.'

PLATO

osmology is the study of the cosmos – the world or the universal order – while psychology studies the psyche or soul, which is the essence of an individual person. As we have seen, in Gnosticism the soul is not the highest or most important aspect of ourselves – that would be the spirit – but it is the most distinctively human. The soul is poised between body and spirit, between the world of matter, which is the world of deficiency, and the Pleroma, which is the world of spirit, of fullness, and in Gnostic schemes it must choose between the two. Thus, the principal division of a human being is into three parts: body, soul and spirit. This threefold division runs though Gnosticism at all levels and in many branches of the tradition and represents the basic predicament of mankind.

In the Manichaean scheme the three creations of man mythically represent spirit, body and soul. The Valentinians also divided humanity as a whole into three categories, according to which aspect was strongest in a person. As we saw in Chapter 2 these were named hylic, after the Greek *hyle* ('matter'), psychic, after *psyche* ('soul'), and pneumatic, after *pneuma* ('spirit'). We will take a further look at Gnostic practices and attitudes regarding the body in Chapter 5.

In modern times there is a tendency to see the body as the only real fact of our existence. Gnostics would have viewed modern science as essentially hylic, and interested only in external, physical phenomena and thus related to the lowest principle within mankind. In its concern with the material and in reducing even the most divine aspects of human existence to a biological level, science might seem to be pleased with that label. Yet the soul is still a concept current to human thinking, however peripheral it may be considered to be to everyday contemporary human life.

We still have notions of spirit too, and though the word may be used in several different ways, it is generally seen as something more abstract, less personal, more *spiritualized* than the soul. For the Gnostics, and for many other religious cultures and philosophies, the distinction between soul and spirit was an important one. The soul was more personal than the spirit – in a sense, what is most typically ourselves. Our ordinary emotions, our passions, our individual thoughts, all belong to the level of the soul. But the spirit exists in a realm beyond that. The soul is still involved in this world, whereas the spirit is akin to the Pleroma and derives from the Pleroma. The spark of light within us is spirit, not soul. From one point of view, the aim of gnosis is to unite the soul with the spirit, and this is the mystical wedding, the rite of the bridal chamber. Ordinarily our souls are united with our bodies and respond to the needs of the body, and, as the *Gospel of Thomas* puts it, 'wretched is the soul that depends on a body'.

According to some Gnostics, the body belongs to matter, which was created and maintained by the archons, and hence parts of the body may be ruled by individual archons. The long version of *The Apocryphon of John* contains a list of body parts and the names of the demons that are associated with them. Perhaps the demons or archons could be appealed to for healing purposes, but these entities are generally hostile to man's spiritual development. In some versions of the Gnostic myth, the body is mere clay, created by the demiurge or by his archons, but inert until the higher life of the soul or spirit is breathed into it.

The state of the hylic, who lives from the body alone, is roughly similar to that of an animal. A hylic is dependent on the body and on the needs and appetites of the body, and the body is incapable of salvation in itself. For the Gnostics there was no bodily resurrection, and they would have agreed with the second-century pagan and anti-Christian philosopher Celsus that the resurrection of a physical corpse was a repugnant concept. Those who live only from the body live in ignorance, which is a lack of gnosis, and gnosis begins with the soul and finds fulfilment in the spirit.

The more extreme Gnostic views on the body may be hard to swallow for many modern readers. After all, for us on earth the body is, despite its limited time span, the most permanent form of identity that we have. Our thoughts may change constantly, feelings come and go, our general sense of ourselves changes with circumstances, even our spiritual experiences are not constant, but the body, despite its aging, is always here for us.

But the Gnostics took the opposite view. What is truly real is gnosis, and the world with which gnosis connects us and from which it derives. The body is the heaviest, least subtle, least real part of ourselves. The Nag Hammadi tractate, *Zostrianos*, gives a brief description of the results of ascetic practice of being separate from the body:

> 'After I parted from the somatic darkness in me and the psychic chaos in mind and the feminine desire [...] in the darkness, I did not use it again. After I found the infinite part of my matter, then I reproved the dead creation within me and the divine Cosmocrater of the perceptible world by preaching powerfully about the All to those with alien parts.'[7]

In my book, *Gnostic Writings on the Soul: Annotated & Explained*, I discuss the history of the soul, and offer a sample of the range of ideas concerning the soul and the spirit that have existed in so many different cultures and religions. The notion of soul is very important to Christianity too, and Gnosticism has influenced certain Christian attitudes to the soul through important Christian theologians such as Clement of Alexandria, Origen and Augustine of Hippo.

The soul is the midpoint between the divine and the animal, and as such it is what is most typically human. And yet, no Gnostic could consider it to be the real Self-with-a-capital-S. Just as in Indian Vedantic teachings, in which the Self is something impersonal, beyond life and death, so in Gnosticism the spirit is part of the Pleroma and, while it might in theory express some distinct quality of the divine, just as the aeons each might express some quality of the ultimate God, the spirit of each human is part of the Pleroma and thus a part of God.

But if the soul is neither divine nor physical, what is it and where does it come from? One Gnostic answer is that the soul was actually created by, or is controlled by, the demiurge and his archons: 'The soul is the food of the archons, without which it cannot live because it derives from the dew above and gives them strength.'[8]

Thus the souls of human beings are part of the created world just as our bodies are. The soul is surely of a finer form of matter than the body is, but it is still not derived from the Pleroma, and many of the difficulties of the human soul – violence, distress, materiality – are the direct result of the soul's origin in the world of the demiurge. In the important Christian Gnostic, possibly Valentinian, work, the *Exegesis on the Soul*, the soul has fallen from the realm of the father.[9] In the *Exegesis*, the soul is feminine and has fallen (without much explanation) from her original residence in the house of the father down into the body in the material world. Once incarnated in a body, the soul falls prey to all sorts of harmful outside influences. She is used as a prostitute and as a result finds herself living with adulterers and thieves (who are probably equivalent to the demonic archons, allegorically representing evil thoughts). She continually gives birth to malformed children (her materialistic thoughts) and lives a wretched existence, caught in a continual cycle of prostitution, abusive relationships and childbearing, until she calls on her father for help. He responds immediately and sends the bridegroom to her. The bridegroom is the spirit, and is both the soul's intended husband and her older brother, esoterically pointing the reader to an understanding that the rejoining of ourselves with the divine element is both a new experience and also the regaining of a lost birthright. Once the soul is in a fit shape, she is wedded to the bridegroom and she finds fulfilment in the bridal chamber.

The *Exegesis* is one of the clearest descriptions of the fall and redemption of the soul, and of the relationship between the soul, the body and the spirit. It is also notable for its allegorical use of passages from the Bible, from the prophets to Paul, which are interpreted as referring to the different stages of the soul's progress, from the soul's fall to the anguish of understanding her situation, to the forgiveness of her father and her marriage with the bridegroom.

A parallel myth, the *Hymn of the Pearl*, describes a similar story from a male point of view. A prince from the East is sent down to Egypt (matter) to bring back a pearl, which is guarded by a serpent. But the prince fails to rescue the pearl when he arrives in Egypt and is lulled into forgetting his quest by the heavy food that he is offered and by the material culture of the Egyptians. He falls asleep and becomes like the Egyptians and has to be reminded of his quest by a letter sent from his homeland. He then awakens to his original aim, promptly takes the pearl from the serpent and returns home, where he is reunited with his kinsmen, including his older brother, and has his glorious robe returned to him.

Here the prince represents the soul, and the pearl, the robe and the older brother all represent the spirit. The story has a strong resemblance to the parable of the prodigal son, which is itself a tale of fall and redemption and would surely have been interpreted by Gnostics as being another allegory of the soul.

Clearly, the soul has two poles of existence: it may be

completely merged with the body and identify itself with the body, while at the other extreme it is permanently united with the spirit in the bridal chamber, and may exist in the Pleroma in the presence of the true God. In the *Hypostasis of the Archons*, a Sethian text discussed earlier, the body was created by the archons, whereas the soul was breathed in by Ialdabaoth. *The Authoritative Teaching* sums it up, 'When the spiritual soul was cast into the body, it became a brother to lust and envy and hatred, and a material soul.'[10]

But there are many states in between these two extremes. The soul can understand its impoverished life and mourn its state. This may be akin to experiencing remorse, an emotional valuation of right and wrong and an understanding of how to proceed, how to move away from absorption in the realm of matter towards the realm of spirit.

The association of the soul with the demiurge also allows us to make a link between the cosmology and psychology.

Gnostic cosmology and psychology are identical in purpose, or at least interlocking. Cosmology describes the universe from an external perspective, psychology from an internal viewpoint. Essentially there is no difference between the two. Just as the world of matter is furthest away from the true God and the Pleroma, so the body is the furthest away from spirit and the Pleroma.

If our souls are not connected to our spirits, then our souls are controlled by the random whims and passions that result from the demands of the body, and we are in a sense our own petty demiurges, ordering our internal world in ignorance of anything higher than ourselves. Our egos then create our own personal worlds out of ignorance and arrogance, with no awareness of any principle that is higher than us. We each say that we are the only God, because we are ignorant of any higher God (which, to take its most immediate manifestation, is the spirit). Thus the higher worlds, the Pleroma, are within us, and yet not only within an individual human, but potentially within each human being. In this sense, the true Self is God, and this is ultimately the same for everyone. Whether we can ever experience the truly highest sense of Self in this earthly life may be disputed, but we can certainly experience the Spirit and, by extension, the Pleroma.

* * *

The spirit must necessarily be described less specifically than the body or the soul, using the same principles in which the Gnostics described God in the negative, specifying what he is not rather than what he is. The spirit may be 'life-giving', 'intellectual' or 'holy', but its qualities are only described in the abstract. In some Gnostic systems, the spirit is an aeon itself, emphasizing that the spirit of an individual human could have a place in the Pleroma. The spirit, and particularly the marriage of soul and spirit, is the fulfilment of gnosis. Its relation to the soul and body is well described in the *Apocryphon of James*:

> 'For without the soul, the body does not sin, just as the soul is not saved without the spirit. But if the soul is saved [when it is] without evil, and the spirit is also saved, then the body becomes free from sin. For it is the spirit that raises the soul, but the body that kills it; that is, it is it which kills itself.'[11]

As ever, the Gnostics had more than one way to crack a nut, and parallel to the myth of the soul's fall from grace and return to the bridegroom the Gnostic used the practice of the ascent of the soul. The ascent of the soul is a visionary journey of the soul from this world back to its source. The process is pictured as an inner journey, an ascent that passes through the different planetary spheres, each of which has different characteristics and places different demands on the soul of the Gnostic.

In Gnostic astrology, the planets correspond to the level of the soul, and their influence on the soul is akin to that of the archons. Hence planetary influence is not to be desired, and freedom from the planets is freedom from the malign influence of Fate. In many Gnostic texts, the Ogdoad, or the eighth level, represents a sphere that is beyond the influence of the planets. The twentieth-century Gnostic scholar Hans Jonas commented, 'The doctrine of the soul's ascent through the spheres... is one of the most constant common features in otherwise widely divergent Gnostic systems.'

We find the ascent of the soul in Hermetic literature, in Sethian and Valentinian literature, in Manichaean and Mandaean practice. It is fundamental to Kabbalah and is perhaps found in the mysteries of Mithras too (see Origen's description in *Contra Celsum* of a Mithraic diagram that resembles the spheres through which the Gnostic must ascend).

There are two aspects of the ascent of the soul. It is often described as the actual journey that the soul travels after death and is particularly important in that aspect in the Mandaean tradition. But it could also be experienced in this life, and as such was:

> 'A psychological technique of inner transform-
> ations by which the self, while still in the body,
> might attain the absolute as an imminent, if
> temporary, condition. An ascending scale of
> mental states replaces the stations of the
> mythical itinerary; the dynamics of progressive
> spiritual self-transformation replaces the special
> thrust through the heavenly spheres.'[12]

In a further allegorization, it might be considered that the planetary archons are an encoding of the dangers that the soul could suffer from the archons in the form of internal thoughts, much like the 'sins' or 'demons' that plague the desert fathers.

Paul's famous experience in 1 Corinthians could serve as a model to Gnostics:

> 'I knew of a man in Christ, about fourteen years
> ago, such was caught up to the third heaven:
> and I knew such a man, who whether in the
> body or out of the body, I cannot tell, how that
> he was caught up into paradise, and heard
> unspeakable words, which it is not possible for
> a man to utter.'

The Nag Hammadi *Apocalypse of Paul* translates this ascension into the spirit:

> 'And then the seventh heaven opened and we
> went up to the Ogdoad, And I saw the twelve
> apostles. They greeted me, and we went up to
> the ninth heaven. I greeted those who were in

the ninth heaven, and we went up to the tenth
heaven. And I greeted my fellow spirits.'

In the *Books of Jeu*, the instructions seem to be explicitly
magical:

'When you come forth from the body and reach
the first aeon, and the archons of that aeon
appear before you, seal yourselves with this seal:
this is its name: *Zōzezēe*, say it but once, seize
this number, 1119, with your two hands.'[13]

In the *Gospel of Mary* the soul ascends past powers such as
darkness, desire and ignorance. The powers attempt to
persuade the soul that it belongs to the material world. Desire
tells the soul that it did not the see the soul ascending – that is,
it tries to persuade the soul that it originated in the material
world, not in the spiritual world. Ignorance tries to persuade
the soul that it is bound to the material world by its nature, and
so on. The names of these allegorical characters and the appeals
that they make to the soul indicate the forces that resist the
soul's ascent. In the *Gospel of Mary* the ascent indicates the
practical efforts that the soul must make to avoid being held
back by the restraining forces.

Irenaeus preserves a long description of the Valentinian
rite of redemption that is intended to guide the soul through its
after-death journey:

'Others still there are who continue to redeem
persons even up to the moment of death, by
placing on their heads oil and water, or the

pre-mentioned ointment with water, using at the
same time the above-named invocations, that the
persons referred to may become incapable of being
seized or seen by the principalities and powers, and
that their inner man may ascend on high in an
invisible manner, as if their body were left among
created things in this world, while their soul is sent
forward to the Demiurge. And they instruct them,
on their reaching the principalities and powers, to
make use of these words: "I am a son from the
Father – the Father who had a pre-existence, and a
son in Him who is pre-existent. I have come to
behold all things, both those which belong to
myself and others, although, strictly speaking, they
do not belong to others, but to Achamoth, who is
female in nature, and made these things for herself.
For I derive being from Him who is pre-existent,
and I come again to my own place whence I went
forth." And they affirm that, by saying these
things, he escapes from the powers.

He then advances to the companions of the
Demiurge, and thus addresses them: "I am a vessel
more precious than the female who formed you. If
your mother is ignorant of her own descent, I
know myself, and am aware whence I am, and I
call upon the incorruptible Sophia, who is in the
Father, and is the mother of your mother, who has
no father, nor any male consort; but a female
springing from a female formed you, while
ignorant of her own mother, and imagining that

she alone existed; but I call upon her mother."
And they declare that when the companions of
the Demiurge hear these words, they are greatly
agitated, and upbraid their origin and the race of
their mother. But he goes into his own place,
having thrown [off] his chain, that is, his animal
nature.'[14]

To what extent was the ascent of the soul visualized and experienced? Visions after all are still mental forms, even if they are
experienced more directly and with a greater sense of reality.
Visions are an indication of reality, even a description of reality,
not a direct experience of reality in the way that a unitive
experience is, yet visions can also be accompanied – necessarily
are – by a different sense of oneself, by gnosis.

In the study of Gnostic psychology the notion of the
Anthropos, from the Greek word *anthropos* which means
humanity, or mankind or humankind – man in the sense of a
human, not in the sense of a human of the male gender – has a
central importance. In many versions of the Gnostic myth, the
anthropos is either one of the aeons, or an even more significant
figure. Man is therefore one of the gods. But why should this be?

The anthropos is the notion of the ideal perfected human and
as such man is one of the immortal characteristics of God. The
perfected spiritual model of man exists endlessly in the Pleroma,
but we humans on earth do not consist only of this ideal
archetype but are the result of subsequent and lower re-
creations.

When Adam is created by the demiurge, in many Gnostic
texts the spiritual Adam is used as a model for the imperfect

creation of the bodily Adam or the psychic Adam. Thus although
we might be fallen individuals, our bodies and souls created by
the demiurge and his archons, in the innermost part of us we are
divine and we share that divinity with the rest of the aeons, and
even with God. According to this idea, an individual person
has something within that originates from beyond the creator of
this world, and thus the archons and demiurge may be disturbed
at the realization that their creation of the modelled form of
man has allowed divinity to enter the world, and so be hostile to
humanity. The concept of the anthropos is one way of relating
human beings to the highest levels of the universe, and in this
sense the Gnostics were far from pessimistic about mankind's
spiritual possibilities.

This all leads us back to the identification of cosmology with
anthropology with psychology. The Gnostic creation descends
from the oneness of God down to the variety of the aeons, then
into the creation of the material world, the human soul that
responds to the material world, and the body which is made of
clay, akin to the lowest level of matter. The aim of the Gnostic is
to exist not merely in the body, or even in the soul, but to use the
soul to contact the spirit.

On the cosmological level, the body belongs to matter and is
ruled by the archons; the soul is ruled by the demiurge and the
archons, while the spirit partakes of the substance of the Pleroma
and the aeons. The heresiologist Hippolytus made this explicit
when he commented that among some Gnostics 'the Sophia is
called "pneuma", the demiurge "soul".' This ties in with the
creation of man, in which the body is often created by the
archons, the soul is breathed in by the demiurge, but it falls upon
Sophia (or another delegate from the Pleroma) to infuse spirit

into the human being and fully animate him. As the great Gnostic scholar Kurt Rudolph put it: 'The "true" or "inner man", "spirit" (*pneuma*) "soul" or "reason" (*nous*) is, over against the body which encloses him, in the same situation as the whole man over against the cosmos.'[15]

Therefore, the demiurge may be considered as being something within us, and the Gnostic myth may be read psychologically. The ignorant, arrogant demiurge is concerned with maintaining this material world, with the things of this world. In this light, the elaborate, extravagant myths of the Gnostics are suddenly seen to be immediately relevant to the human condition. Perhaps the classic Gnostic myths were not evidence of a world-hating mentality, as so many enemies of the Gnostics have claimed, but represent a penetrating insight into human psychology.

CHAPTER 4

UPSIDE DOWN AND INSIDE OUT: THE GNOSTIC INTERPRETATION OF THE BIBLE

'Both read the bible day and night,
But you read black where I read white!'

WILLIAM BLAKE

The Gnostics created their own writings in abundance, but they never created a canon of texts, or endowed their own creations with the status of official scripture. They never did put together their own Bible, but instead reinterpreted the Hebrew Bible and the emerging Christian scriptures, the gospels and epistles that were to be gathered together as the New Testament.[16]

In the early centuries CE, there were Jewish Christian groups like the Ebionites and Nazarenes who kept Torah law, yet believed that Jesus was the Jewish messiah. But on the whole there is much in the Hebrew Bible that is specific to the Jewish people, that neither Christians nor Gnostics could accommodate in their religions. The eventual Christian response to the Hebrew Bible was to declare it the Old Testament and to reject any aspects of it that could not apply to Christians as being no longer part of God's covenant with mankind. The Jews had failed God, the Christians declared, and Christ had come to set that right and to offer a new covenant with God that was open to those who would declare Christ as their saviour. Inconvenient cultural strictures like the circumcision requirement and the food laws were irrelevant now that God's covenant was with Christians, not Jews.

The Gnostics took a different approach − in fact, two different approaches, inverse exegesis and allegorical interpretation. Inverse exegesis is an upside-down interpretation because it tips the established interpretation on its head. Allegorical interpretation is inside out because the inner spiritual meaning of a passage is considered more important than the outer literal meaning. The first approach is familiar to us from the Gnostic interpretations of Genesis that we looked at in Chapter 2. The Gnostics identified the Jewish God with the lower God, the demiurge, who was ignorant, arrogant or malicious, and hence any episode in the Hebrew Bible could be read through the technique of inverse exegesis.

Any prophet who did the bidding of Yahweh was a servant of the demiurge, not a divine revealer. Moses was particularly a victim of this approach and, as the revealer or architect of the Torah law (and in ancient times Moses was believed to have composed the entire Torah, and the first five books of the Bible, even though his own death is reported therein), was the principal agent of the demiurge, and thus had no mitigating qualities. Hence, the Gnostic exegesis inverted the conventional meaning of the scripture and made the God of the Hebrews into an enemy of mankind.

Other biblical figures could be treated more ambiguously. Adam and Eve could be treated more sympathetically in Gnostic accounts because they were victims of the lower God, not the transgressing sinners of the usual interpretations. Marginal figures like Seth or Melchizedek could be promoted into Gnostic heroes, the very lack of explicit scriptural tradition allowing them to be completely re-imagined within a Gnostic framework.

In the *Apocryphon of John*, the author repeatedly states, 'It is not as Moses said', and minor details of the creation account are reinterpreted in the light of Gnostic teaching. In the *Second Treatise of the Great Seth*, Moses, like Adam, Abraham, Isaac and Jacob, is even described as a 'laughing stock'. Inverse exegesis is a particularly powerful method for those who are already familiar with the tradition. The First World War poet Wilfred Owen used it to great effect in his poem 'The Parable of the Young Man and the Old'. The bulk of this poem is a straight retelling of the story of Abraham's sacrifice of Isaac from Genesis 22, a parable of absolute obedience to a stern but, in the end, merciful God. Until the last two lines, the story is followed faithfully, with a few added specifics that make clear that the First World War is being referenced, and the reader expects Abraham to sacrifice the ram ('of pride' in Owen's interpretation) in place of Isaac.

> 'So Abram rose, and clave the wood, and went,
> And took the fire with him, and a knife.
> And as they sojourned, both of them together,

Isaac the first-born spake, and said, My Father,
Behold the preparations, fire and iron,
But where the lamb for this burnt-offering?
Then Abram bound the youth with belts and straps,
And builded parapets and trenches there,
And stretched forth the knife to slay his son.
When lo! an angel called him out of heaven,
Saying, "Lay not thy hand upon the lad,
Neither do anything to him. Behold,
A ram, caught in a thicket by its horns;
Offer the Ram of Pride instead of him." '

But the last two lines have a sting in the tail:

'But the old man would not so, but slew his son,
And half the seed of Europe, one by one.'

The masterful example of inverse exegesis changes the whole purpose of the story.

* * *

The flood was the subject of a number of Gnostic texts, and the existence of flood stories in other mythologies made this episode especially appealing to Hellenistic Gnostics familiar with pagan mythology. The author of the *Apocalypse of Adam* actually identifies Noah with the Greek Deucalion, the son of Prometheus who survives Zeus' flooding of the world. In the usual reading of the biblical deluge story, Noah is God's champion, preserving the faithful core of an otherwise corrupt humanity by the will of God. To Christians and Jews, Noah was the righteous hero who trusted in God, survived the flood in his ark, and laid the foundation for a new beginning for humanity. In the surviving

Gnostic accounts, Noah is not turned into a Gnostic hero, but is considered to be the tool of the demiurge and his archons, who wish that the demiurgic culture and religion created by them – mainstream Christianity and Judaism – should survive the flood.

In the *Hypostasis of the Archons*, Norea is depicted as being both the daughter of Eve and a female spiritual principle, something of a female equivalent to Seth. The archons have arranged for the flood to occur, and the demiurge helps Noah to survive the flood in the ark. When Norea requests entrance to the ark, she is refused admittance. She responds by burning up the ark, and Noah has to build it again. Then the archons try to rape her, but she calls on the God of the All, who sends Eleleth, one of the four Sethian luminaries, to Norea. At this point, the rest of the story is forgotten and instead the revelations about the creation and humanity that Eleleth gives to Norea are recounted. This sometimes bizarre reworking of the story of Noah and the flood consistently casts Noah as a pawn of the archons, who wish to eradicate the seed of Seth from the world.

In the *Revelation of Adam*, the flood is brought about by the demiurge as a device by which he can eliminate humans who do not serve him. These disobedient humans happen to be the Gnostics, who serve instead the true God and his angels. The great angels of the world of light preserve the Gnostics from the flood, but Noah is also preserved by the demiurge. Thus both sides are frustrated, and the situation after the flood is much the same as that before it. After the flood, the descendants of Seth mate with the descendants of Noah again, reintroducing the seed of Seth and its attendant spirituality into humanity, and this frustrates the aim of the demiurge, who caused the flooding in order to eliminate the influence of Seth from his world.

The above tales of the flood, and the various versions of the creation myth, involve inverse exegesis as a way of subverting the original intent of the Bible. It is no coincidence that the above examples of inverse exegesis are Sethian in authorship. Valentinus and the Valentinians also applied this interpretive method that turned the scriptures topsy-turvy, but more often pressed into service the technique of allegorical interpretation. Allegorical interpretation allows the reader to make the text say something other than its ostensible surface meaning. When people allegorize texts, they are usually convinced that their interpretations actually represent the genuine inner meaning of the text.

But the allegorical approach, or related symbolic or metaphorical techniques, can also be used to compose writings, and the Gnostics and other spiritual movements used myth, symbol and metaphor as their everyday currencies. If the text was originally written using the allegorical method, as a way of encoding spiritual truths in an indirect form, then allegorical interpretation may allow the reader to extract that hidden meaning, and this is, of course, what most people believe that they are doing when they read a text allegorically: they believe that they are reading the text as it is intended to be read.

The allegorical interpretation of the Bible was a respectable tradition in the early centuries CE. When Jewish culture, with its unique religion, met Hellenistic society, with its tradition of philosophy, each side became interested in the traditions of the other culture. Hellenized Jews like Philo of Alexandria admired Plato and Platonic philosophy, and hence read the principles of Platonism into the Bible. On the other side, Hellenistic intellectuals were fascinated by many of the attractive features of Jewish culture, by its monotheism, by the sense of community and high moral standards, and by the ancient scriptures of the Jews, but they also wished to dovetail Jewish beliefs with their own philosophical and religious systems. Among the offshoots of this process were Gnosticism and Christian Platonism, Gnosticism's more respectable sister.

Philo's way of platonizing the Bible, which amounted to interpreting biblical figures, stories and even Torah law in terms of such concepts as the soul, the senses, the virtues, the demiurge and the good, was pressed into use by the Valentinians – the Nag Hammadi text *The Testimony of Truth* particularly shows the influence of Philo.

The Valentinians were also able to interpret the gospels and the epistles esoterically, and they had a special regard for the writings of Paul. The Valentinian *Excerpts from Theodotus* tell us that, 'The Saviour taught the Apostles at first figuratively and mystically, later in parables and riddles, and thirdly clearly and openly when they were alone.'[17]

When we look at the Gnostic interpretations of the gospels, they can be quite surprising. Irenaeus includes some of these as examples of the misleading beliefs of the Gnostics, and while we must take into account that he wishes to emphasize the differences between his form of Christianity and the Gnostic, and always describes Gnostic ideas in as complicated a way as possible, Irenaeus' accounts are probably fairly reliable.

According to the Valentinians, the 30 aeons of the Pleroma are described in the parable of the labourers sent into the vineyard. In the gospel parable, some of the labourers join the crew in the first hour, others around the third hour, the sixth hour, the ninth hour and still others around the eleventh hour.

If these are added up (1+3+6+9+11) the number of labourers totals 30, the number of aeons in the Pleroma. Thus the parable of the labourers is, according to the Valentinians, concerned with the emanation of the aeons and the creation of the Pleroma. The precedence of the labourers presumably refers to the different groupings and importance of the aeons.[18]

Some of the miracle stories in the gospels are heavy with hidden meaning, and many modern scholars believe that they are not genuine accounts, or even distorted accounts, of actual healings, but are principally theological (in the broadest sense) in their message. The miracle stories in the gospels may be more akin to the parables than to any attempt at a historical account. The 30 aeons are discovered once again in the miracle stories, but the number 30 must be split into the numbers 12 and 18. The number 12 is found in Luke, in the age of Jesus when he visited the temple in Jerusalem, and the remaining 18 is in a non-canonical tradition that Jesus remained with his disciples for 18 months after the resurrection, not for the mere 40 days of the canonical account. The numbers from these two stories added together once again (18+12) refer to the 30 Valentinian aeons.

The maiden who suffered from the issue of blood in the miracle of the raising of Jairus' daughter, was 12 years old, and represented the twelfth aeon, Sophia, who stretched out into the immensity (in one version of the fall of Sophia) but was restrained from falling completely by touching the hem of the garment of the Son, which resulted in a lower version of Sophia, named Achamoth, being separated from the higher version. Irenaeus, always keen to convince us of the obscurity of Gnostic doctrine, expresses this in cosmological terms. But if Sophia is understood as being the spirit, then the tale of a 12-year-old girl who appears dead but really is just asleep, can be interpreted quite easily as an allegory of the soul that has fallen asleep by losing contact with the spirit.

A similar numerical interpretation is given for the role of Judas as a disciple. The Valentinians compared Judas to Sophia, the thirteenth aeon in this version, who fell from grace but was eventually redeemed and restored to the Pleroma. The implication is that Judas also fell, but was restored to grace. Irenaeus objects that the comparison is not appropriate because Judas was not redeemed, but was a traitor who paid for the betrayal of Christ by committing suicide. But that is exactly the point: these Gnostics must have believed that Judas was redeemed in order to compare him to the thirteenth aeon, and so the role of Judas as a disciple is an illustration of the fall and redemption of the soul. This obscure passage in Irenaeus is further evidence of a positive view of Judas among Gnostics, albeit in a rarefied cosmological setting.

Once again, the question with allegorical or esoteric interpretation is whether the original intention of the material is being brought out in the interpretation, or whether allegory is being used in an attempt to make the material say something other than was actually meant. We can be very post-modern about this and we can say the interaction between reader and text always involves interpretation, and that a reader can never truly know the intentions of the author, but the question remains (and it is not one that can be addressed fully in this book): were the gospels in particular intended to be interpreted esoterically?

There are certainly many examples of allegory and symbolism in the New Testament. Parables are perhaps the most famous component of the teachings of Jesus in the gospels. If Jesus was anything, he was a teller of parables, and the subtlety of his parables is unmatched. We find clues in the Gospel of Mark, which is seen by most scholars as the earliest gospel, that indicate that the surface meaning of a literal story of a Jesus who gathered disciples, taught them and the multitude and then was crucified, is not the most important level of meaning. Sayings, parables and proverbs are often accompanied by the injunction 'He who has ears to hear, let him hear.' The 12 disciples are told, 'To you it has been given to know the mystery of the kingdom of God; but to those who are outside, all things come in parables' (Mark 4:11).

There is a feeding of the 5,000 and a feeding of the 4,000, and when the second feeding of the multitudes occurs in Mark 8, Jesus explains that there is a hidden meaning to the two feedings, a meaning that is based on number symbolism: on the number of baskets, pieces of fish and bread. David Fideler has argued quite convincingly that both the miracle of the loaves and fishes and the episode at the end of the Gospel of John, in which Simon Peter and the risen Christ catch 153 fish, are based on Pythagorean geometry.[19]

We are told explicitly in the Gospel of Mark that in the parable of the sower, the seed is the Word or Logos, but more often a parable leaves us to find an application for it.

There are many further examples, and though we can never prove in an entirely scholarly manner that the gospels contain a core of Gnostic inner meaning, we, like the Valentinians, may feel that this is indeed the case.

The very earliest parts of the New Testament are the letters of Paul, which are dated to the 40s and 50s of the first century. The relationship between Paul and the Gnostics is one of the most confusing issues in both the origins of Gnosticism and the development of Christianity. Some of Paul's letters suggest an antagonistic relationship to tendencies toward proto-Gnostic elements in Christian groups, and Paul famously writes in 1 Corinthians that 'Knowledge [gnosis] puffs up'. Many scholars have argued that Paul was opposing Gnostic or proto-Gnostic groups and individuals. And yet there are many aspects of Paul's writings that seem very Gnostic.

The second- and third-century Gnostics had less difficulty with the issue of Paul's seemingly divided loyalties than we might. As far as they were concerned, Paul was a Gnostic, the 'great apostle', and the Valentinians were happy to trace their spiritual lineage back to him, via Valentinus' teacher Theudas. The Valentinians quoted Paul's letters often and interpreted them in the light of the Valentinian Gnostic system.

Paul himself was not quite as influential among proto-orthodox Christians during the second century as he was among Valentinians and Marcionites, and the canon of Paul's epistles as included in the New Testament contains spurious letters that are no longer attributed to Paul. It is generally acknowledged that the so-called Pastoral Epistles (1 Timothy, 2 Timothy and Titus) were not written by Paul, this attribution being merely traditional, though the anti-Gnostic Church Father Tertullian insisted on the validity of the Pastoral Epistles. The Pastorals adopt some of the Pauline ideas, but move Paul's thought in the direction of orthodoxy, and the inclusion of the Pastorals in the New Testament, and the ordering of Paul's letters by their length in descending order give a false impression of Paul's own thought.

Paul is rarely translated as if he is a Gnostic, and terminology that seems very Gnostic in the Greek is usually rendered into English in a way that minimizes this.

For instance, 1 Corinthians 2:6–8:

> 'Yet among the mature we do speak of Sophia, though it is not the Sophia of this aeon or of the archons of this aeon, who are doomed to perish. But we speak of the holy Sophia, secret and hidden, which God decreed before the aeons for our glory. None of the archons of this aeon understood this.'

At first glance this could be an extract from any Gnostic text, and it is obviously straightforward for a Gnostic to interpret. Indeed, it almost needs no interpretation and would require a particularly non-Gnostic frame of mind in order to treat it in any other way. Theodotus the Valentinian stated that Paul 'taught in two ways at once':[20] on the one hand proclaiming Christ 'according to the flesh' as a man or God who was crucified and raised; and on the other hand according to the spirit. Much of the Valentinian interpretation of Paul focused on the difference between hylics, those of matter; psychics, those of the soul, who are the ordinary Christians; and pneumatics, Gnostics, those who have the spirit in addition to the soul. By extension, to speak about the hylics, psychics and pneumatics is to speak about the body, soul and spirit themselves.

But not all of the Gnostic interpretations of Paul were so justifiable. We might think that the early Gnostic Basilides was forcing the issue a little when, according to Origen, he claimed that Paul's statement that 'I was once alive apart from the law' (Romans 7:9) refers to reincarnation or metempsychosis, because

Paul (and the rest of us) lived in the body of an animal or bird in a previous lifetime, and that the life of an animal, not being human, was not subject to the law.[21] Paul himself perhaps had a Jekyll and Hyde quality, containing both the most literalist Christian tendencies and the most Gnostic.

The story of Judas receives a reinterpretation from a Gnostic perspective in the *Gospel of Judas*, which famously resurfaced in Codex Tchacos, a Coptic Gnostic codex which seems to have been discovered in the 1970s. It was subsequently touted at a ridiculously high price to a group of academics, then disappeared again and was kept in a humid New York State safe deposit box, sold, frozen, snapped in two, sold back, assessed at Yale Library, rejected by Yale, and then finally purchased by *National Geographic*, who restored it, monopolized it, ignored scholarly protocol and created a media bonanza out of this ancient text.

Initially, the *Gospel of Judas* was presented as clearly being the same one described by Irenaeus, attributed by him to a Sethian-style group who:

> 'Declare that Cain derived his being from the
> Power above, and acknowledge that Esau, Korah,
> the Sodomites and all such persons, are related to
> themselves ... They declare that Judas the traitor
> was thoroughly acquainted with these things,
> and that he alone, knowing the truth as no others
> did, accomplished the mystery of the betrayal; by
> him all things, both earthly and heavenly, were
> thus thrown into confusion. They produce a
> fictional history of this kind, which they style
> the Gospel of Judas.'

The method of inverse exegesis will be familiar from Irenaeus' account. Whether Irenaeus knew of a different *Gospel of Judas* that matched his account or whether he misinterpreted the *Gospel of Judas* from Codex Tchacos is unclear. Indeed, its interpretation is now up in the air, and whether the *Gospel of Judas* actually does represent Judas as a hero, or whether he, as a betrayer of Jesus, is merely a typical example of the disciples of Jesus, is a debatable point. Although it is not beyond possibility, historical analysis suggests that this gospel does not preserve independent historical information about Judas, and anyway, as we have seen, the Gnostics were not much concerned with history, not even with their own histories.

Instead, the *Gospel of Judas* is a reinterpretation of an existing story, just as we find with the Gnostic versions of the Adam and Eve, Noah and other biblical stories. It is perhaps inversionary in its view of Judas, and if not, at least in its view of the disciples. Scholar Stephen Emmel compared the *Gospel of Judas* to Stoppard's *Rosencrantz and Guildenstern Are Dead*, which takes the characters from Shakespeare's *Hamlet* and reads between the lines to give us a back-story that puts the events of the play in a different light. The *Gospel of Judas* does something similar, filling in the blanks of the familiar story from the four gospels, and reading between the lines to give us background information.

* * *

Of the dozens of tractates in the NHL, it is the *Gospel of Thomas* that has demanded the most immediate attention, and from its first publication in translation in 1959 to the current day it has caught the interest of the public and academia alike. The *Gospel of Thomas* is a collection of the sayings of Jesus, mostly preceded by a simple, 'Jesus said', sometimes with a sentence or two to provide context or occasionally a short dialogue between Jesus and a questioner, or one disciple and another. Some sayings are very similar to those found in Matthew, Mark and Luke, the synoptic gospels, while others are previously unknown.

Many of the familiar sayings, though, are subtly different to the versions that we know. It is partly the lack of a story context that makes them different, but also they have a more esoteric turn to them, and there are strange references to making two into one or revealing what is hidden. Of the unfamiliar sayings some, such as this one, Number 8, from the *Gospel of Thomas*:

> 'The kingdom is like a wise fisherman who cast
> his net into the sea; then he drew it up from the
> sea, full of little fish from below. Among them he
> found one good large fish. So he threw all of the
> little fish back down into the sea without regret'

could easily fit into the New Testament, while others such as Number 7, 'Blessed is the lion that the man consumes, and the lion becomes man', are more mysterious.

However, even though the *Gospel of Thomas* was discovered at Nag Hammadi with other Gnostic writings, is it truly a Gnostic gospel? This question has been crucial to *Thomas* studies since academics first investigated it. Most modern commentators would now take the view that *Thomas* isn't a full-blown Gnostic gospel – that is, it is not a product of the Sethians and Valentinians, who we know existed by the second century. Despite the fact that it was found with other Gnostic texts, some would deny that it is Gnostic at all, especially considering that there are also fragments of *Thomas* from three different copies in Greek which are earlier than the Nag Hammadi Library Coptic translation and which were not found in a Gnostic context.

Nag Hammadi Codex II, which is where we find the *Gospel of Thomas*, starts with the *Apocryphon of John*, the classic text of Sethian Gnosticism, then continues with the *Gospel of Thomas*, and also contains the Valentinian *Gospel of Philip* and hardcore Gnostic texts like the *Origin of the World*. So we can be certain that the *Gospel of Thomas* was interpreted Gnostically, at least by the people who compiled and read Codex II.

Sayings like Number 28 would have been understood instantly by Gnostics:

> 'I rose up within the world and I appeared outwardly to them in the flesh. I found them all drunk and I found none of them thirsty, and my soul was pained for the sons of men, for they are blind in their hearts and do not see. For they came into the world empty, and seek also to go out of the world empty. But now they are drunk. When they shake off their wine, their hearts will change.'[22]

Yet in many ways the *Gospel of Thomas* deserves to be dated as early as the synoptic gospels, and is a potential source of genuine sayings of Jesus.

What kind of Gnosticism could have produced the *Gospel of Thomas*? *Thomas* doesn't look Sethian; it has neither the layered complexity of Sethian texts, nor the convention-turning ethos. It may have some similarity to Valentinian texts, with its parables and metaphors and its encouragement to esoteric interpretation ('whoever understands the meaning of these sayings shall not taste death'). The compiler of the Valentinian *Gospel of Philip* may well have known the *Gospel of Thomas* since a good half dozen sayings from *Thomas* appear in *Philip*. Several different literary developments have been proposed for *Thomas*: that *Thomas* originated as a smaller core of sayings that are held in common with the synoptics and then was redacted (edited) in a Gnostic direction;[23] that *Thomas* was a rolling corpus,[24] again beginning with a core that was close to the synoptic sayings, but then having material added to it as it was copied and moved location.

If we look for the locations where *Thomas* was written we find suggestions of Jerusalem for the core, then Egypt and, more often, Syria, both classic Gnostic countries. All of the surviving copies of *Thomas*, in Greek and Coptic, were found in Egypt, which is largely a function of Egypt's exceptionally dry climate, but Syria has a strong tradition of texts connected with the name of Thomas.

The *Gospel of Thomas* is named after Didymos Judas Thomas, who may be identified with the Doubting Thomas of John's gospel. Didymos means 'twin' in Greek, Judas means 'twin' in Aramaic. An ancient tradition placed Thomas in Syria – his body was reputedly deposited in a tomb there, and a forged correspondence between Jesus and Abgarus, king of Syria, recommended Thomas as a visiting apostle to the king. The apocryphal Acts of Thomas also connects Thomas with Syria. There are indeed signs that there was a Thomasine Christianity that was connected with Syrian ascetic Christianity, a form of Christianity that could appeal to Gnostics but was not part of the main river of Gnosticism.

* * *

The crucifixion and resurrection of Jesus Christ are at the core of Christian belief, but were not central to Gnostic systems. Gnostic views of the crucifixion and resurrection of Jesus fall roughly into

two camps. One, which is more Valentinian, emphasizes resurrection as a spiritual resurrection, based strongly on an interpretation
of Paul. Thus, resurrection may be experienced in this life, as the
Gospel of Philip 19 puts it: 'Those who say that the Lord first died
and then arose are confused, for he first arose and then died.
Anyone who first acquires the resurrection shall not die.'[25]

This spiritual resurrection is of course another way of looking
at gnosis. When we lack gnosis we are spiritually dead, but
when we experience gnosis we rise from the dead. Thus the
story of Jesus could be used as a model for inner spiritual
experience, just as it was, though with a more literal element, for
the great Christian mystics of the Orthodox and Catholic
traditions. In undergoing a crucifixion and resurrection the
Christian mystic imitates Christ.

The other typically Gnostic attitude towards the crucifixion
and resurrection treats the crucifixion as an illusion. Jesus never
actually had a physical body, and thus he could not have been
crucified and the crucifixion was an illusion. This view is termed
Docetism, from the Greek verb *dokeo*, to show. The Valentinian
Interpretation of Knowledge contains a particularly stinging
rebuke of the orthodox Christian focus on the crucifixion:

> 'And he was crucified and he died – not his own
> death, for he did not at all deserve to die because
> of the church of mortals. And he was nailed so
> that they might keep him in the Church.'

The literal crucifixion and resurrection are so fundamental to
orthodox Christianity that modern Christianity could not exist
without them. The focus on the crucifixion is, in its extremes,
a morbid one and there is something in the notion of the

vicarious sacrifice of Jesus that detracts from a genuine personal spirituality. Mainstream Christians were anxious to assert that Jesus really did have a physical body, and was really incarnated, as in Ignatius' late first-century Epistle to the Thrallians:

> 'Close your ears, then, if anyone preaches to you
> without speaking of Jesus Christ. Christ was of
> David's line. He was the son of Mary, who was
> really born, ate and drank, was really persecuted
> under Pontius Pilate, was really crucified...
> He was also truly raised from the dead.'[26]

In *The Second Treatise of the Great Seth*, and also in an account of Basilides by Irenaeus, an actual mechanism by which Jesus may have avoided crucifixion is suggested. In the canonical gospels, Simon of Cyrene carried Jesus' cross for him, but in the Sethian and Basilidean accounts, Simon was crucified instead of Jesus, who rather unkindly stood by laughing as he watched it happen. Docetism also crops up in later Gnostic movements, in the theology of the Bogomils and Cathars.

* * *

Herakleon, a follower of Valentinus, wrote the first substantial commentary on a gospel, which survives only in extract in a refutation by Origen. Origen's interaction with Herakleon's commentary seems to have prompted him to develop his own commentary on John, which proved to be very influential. Some aspects of Herakleon's interpretation would not seem out of place in an orthodox Christian allegory, but others refer explicitly to the Gnostic cosmology. Sometimes the interpretations seem quite forced, but no more than Origen's in his commentary. The Gospel of John itself is somewhat Gnostic in nature, and it was the most popular gospel for many Gnostics – the medieval Cathars, for example, prized John above the other gospels. Theodotus interprets, 'Thus when he says "I am the door," he means that you, who are of the superior seed, shall come up to the boundary where I am.'[27]

The Gospel of John may have been influenced by Gnostic or proto-Gnostic ideas, or alternatively may have been written as an attempt to refute Gnostic concepts like Docetism and to provide an orthodox challenge to them.

Techniques of allegorical interpretation were preserved by Christianity by the intellectual tradition that began with Clement of Alexandria and Origen. Augustine of Hippo produced a notorious interpretation of the parable of the Good Samaritan, full of eisegesis (reading something *into* the text, rather than exegesis, teasing the meaning *out of* the text) in which every single element of the parable mirrors something in Church doctrine; he even goes so far as to state that the apostle Paul is the innkeeper in the parable.

* * *

Much ink has been spent on the question of whether the Gnostics preserved secret knowledge of the historical Jesus, for instance whether Jesus and Mary Magdalene were married, or whether Jesus survived the crucifixion (as he must have done if it was Simon of Cyrene who was crucified instead of him), or whether Judas was Jesus' most trusted disciple. Certainly, all of these views are represented in Gnostic texts, but along with the academic scholars I do not suspect that they were preserving streams of historical fact –the Gnostics had little enough interest in their own origins – but reinterpreting and challenging the received view of Christianity.

Which is not to say that the proto-orthodox views of the life of Jesus and the origins of the Church were necessarily more historical. Rigorous historical criticism of the gospels has dismantled Jesus to such an extent that it is difficult to put him back together again. The Gnostic heresy of Docetism has received a modern revival in the work of writers such as Earl Doherty, Timothy Freke and Peter Gandy, and G.A. Wells, who have presented strong arguments that there never was a historical Jesus who founded Christianity. Perhaps those Gnostics were not speaking entirely about spiritual matters when they stated that Jesus never had a real physical body!

The Gnostics were not particularly interested in the biography of Jesus. Did they then believe that he had never existed in a literal sense, had never been incarnated on earth? The two notions are not identical. Jesus may have been considered to have actually existed and manifested without an ordinary physical body. That is, he was considered to have existed on earth in a literal and not metaphorical sense even if he did not have an ordinary physical body.

In the late twentieth century a number of alternative scholars such as G.A. Wells, Earl Doherty, Tim Freke and Peter Gandy, Alvar Ellegard, Robert Price and, in a less scholarly fashion, Acharya S., have argued that there never actually was a historical person named Jesus who was the founder of the Christian religion and the character described in the gospels. The most rigorous of these is Earl Doherty, who writes entirely from a secular, humanistic, atheist background.

Tim Freke and Peter Gandy are less rigorous but write from a genuinely Gnostic point of view. Doherty has taken the tendencies of modern academic investigation of the historical

Jesus to its logical extreme. Critical investigation of the gospels and their proposed sources suggest that there is little in the life of Jesus that can be considered to be truly historical. This is the nature of our sources, which are not independent accounts and were not written in a spirit of historical investigation but for religious purposes (though the Gnostics would disagree with modern scholars on what those purposes were.) Any claim to historicity in the gospels requires a sophisticated sifting of evidence and the use of a methodology or of specific criteria by which historicity may be assessed.

By now, the gospels have been deconstructed to such an extent that there is little left – perhaps just the 'fact' of the crucifixion and some connection between the apostles of the early Church and the Jesus of the gospels.

Earlier than the gospels are the letters of Paul. Paul seems to know little about Jesus other than that he was crucified. And Paul's Jesus bears a distinct resemblance to the dying and rising god who was central to some of the Hellenistic pagan mystery religions. Perhaps, as Doherty or Freke and Gandy have argued, there was never a historical Jesus at all, but Christianity originated as a kind of mystery cult. (Wells, Ellegard and, earlier, G.R.S. Mead believed that the earliest Christians thought of Jesus as having lived generations before them.)

The Gnostic understanding of the mission of Jesus was quite different to the mainstream Christian or Catholic understanding. It was not the founding of the Church that was the most important aspect of Jesus' time on earth, nor was his bodily resurrection his most significant act. Jesus brought gnosis, and the significance of his time on earth was as a revealer of knowledge.

CHAPTER 5

PRAXIS:
WHAT DID THE GNOSTICS
ACTUALLY DO?

Anyone who is interested in the Gnostics will naturally ask, 'Well, what did the Gnostics actually *do*?' If an ancient Gnostic had been asked this question, he may well have answered, 'It is not what we do, but what we *know* that is important. This is what sets us apart from others.'

That is, it is not *praxis* ('action'), nor *pistis* ('faith'), but *gnosis* that is truly important for Gnostics. This is indeed so, but no people on earth can survive by knowledge alone. In any spiritual discipline, even in the most direct approach to God, there is always an element of practice, of technique, of spiritual exercise, and this was true for the Gnostics too.

Knowledge can have a transformative quality in itself, and if the principles of Gnosticism touch us personally, we can never see the world in the same way again. But knowledge must be applied to life, not held separately from our experience as a mere philosophy. True knowledge is direct, personal knowing –

acquaintance, recognition, familiarity with God, knowing God as one might know an ideal father or mother or friend or lover. Practices are external, but experience is an internal quality and Gnosis is an inner quality. For Gnostics, the external world is the created world, the world of matter, the world in which the body lives. Within us is the soul, which belongs to the external world, at least in its unspiritualized state. Spiritual practices and disciplines provide fixed forms that exist in the material worlds yet affect our souls in the inner world in order to connect our souls to our spirits and the transcendent world of the Pleroma. Thus spiritual practices relate to the level of the soul, providing a form in which the soul can reach out to the spirit.

The various interruptions in the transmission of Gnostic teaching mean that no rituals or techniques have been handed down to us from Gnostic to Gnostic to our modern world, so modern Gnostic praxis is either derived from the descriptions given in ancient Gnostic texts or in the heresiologists, or otherwise uses practices from other traditions. Modern Gnostics have used Zen and other forms of Buddhism, theosophy, Orthodox or Catholic Christianity, the Western occult tradition, Gurdjieff's Fourth Way and Jungianism, amongst others, to interpret Gnosticism, and have thus borrowed practices from these other traditions, or used the direct experience of these traditions as a key with which to understand and recreate Gnostic experience. In this chapter I will focus on the historically attested techniques of the ancient Gnostics.[28]

Gnostics felt that the body is born of pain and it will die in the same way. It hungers, thirsts, needs shelter, craves sex, power, possessions, comfort, excitement, and can be a tyrant. It is a kind of animal. It is a coat or garment that is put on and taken off and our true identity does not lie in the body. 'The body is a temporary dwelling which the rulers and authorities have as an abode.'[29]

If the body is the lowest part of the trichotomy of body, soul and spirit that comprises a human being, how should it be treated? The body of a pneumatic is identical to that of a psychic or a hylic, it is the activity of the soul and spirit that makes the difference. Gnostics can approach the body in three ways. The first way is that of moderation, the golden mean derived from the classical ideal. A Gnostic treats his or her body normally, avoiding extremes of indulgence and restraint. The body should be fed moderately, clothed, exercised, disciplined, healed when it is sick. It should be treated well, yet should not take up too much importance in life. The customs and the diet of our own cultures should be followed – it is not what goes into the mouth that defiles it, but what comes out of it.

The two other approaches are attested in Gnostic or heresiological literature, and are considered more distinctively Gnostic. These are the two poles of asceticism and libertinism. Neither of these extremes was universally held, nor was even necessarily typical, among Gnostics, and extremes of bodily denial or indulgence were not, in the ancient world, restricted to Gnostics; witness the twin philosophies of the Stoics and Epicureans, who respectively denied the body and indulged it. Christianity itself has a long and persistent tradition of ascetic practices, among which may be included celibacy, despite the protestations of many Christian theologians that the body is created good, as is the world.

In the last decade or so, scholars like Michael Allen Williams[30] have challenged the previously held notions of the extent of asceticism in the Gnostics. Gnostic asceticism was not nearly as widely attested as many commentators had assumed, but it certainly is an element of Gnostic practice.

For the ascetically inclined, the most problematic aspects of the body are not illness or lack of comfort, but the physical appetites and desires. Fasting, physical endurance and restricting the hours of sleep are all classic ways in which the body may be disciplined. Fasting is itself fairly well represented in Gnostic texts. Some Gnostics, such as the followers of Satornilos, abstained from meat, while other Gnostic sects were criticized for eating meat that had been sacrificed to pagan idols. (In the ancient world all butchery was performed in a religious context, as is the case with halal or kosher butchery today.) Food, especially meat, was widely thought to make the soul sluggish, or to increase sexual desire, and in the *Hymn of the Pearl*, the prince falls asleep when he accepts the food of the Egyptians.

Extended fasting is often accompanied by euphoria and a feeling of lightness and physical purity, all of which would be perceived as enabling a connection with the spirit and with the divine. The *Gospel of Thomas* is ambiguous about fasting, at one point declaring in 14, 'If you fast, you will bring sin on yourselves'; and in 27, 'If you do not fast from the world, you will not find the kingdom.' Sometimes, 'fasting' is used figuratively by Gnostics to mean abstaining from certain aspects of the physical world. Wine was avoided by some Gnostics and the Gnostic teacher Severus was said by Epiphanius to have instructed his students to avoid both wine and sexual intercourse; the latter was to be avoided even in marriage.

Perhaps the most spiritually challenging of the body's appetites is that which hungers for sex. Sex is unique among the bodily functions, both in its biological role and its intensity. It is the only bodily function that transcends itself and the only function that requires the involvement of another person, the only truly creative aspect of the body. Through sex two bodies can create a new physical body and bring another soul into the material world. But human sexuality involves more than mere procreation. Sexuality – and perhaps particularly male sexuality – can become distorted, and can take over a life. From the Gnostic point of view it can bind the soul to matter, making the inner life a slave to physical urges. Many a promising modern guru has been brought low by his inability to balance his sex life.

There were many models for sexuality in the ancient world. The family unit remained strong in Hellenistic culture, and in most traditional societies sexual activity was formalized into cultural patterns of courtship, marriage, childbearing and child rearing. Jewish sexuality typically emphasized the duty of parents to bear children, to go forth and multiply. But there were also strongly promiscuous aspects to Hellenistic society. Men have always been in an advantageous position in casual relationships because they can beget but not conceive, and can leave the fruit of their loins behind with the female partner. Prostitutes were in constant danger of conceiving and having to abort their children (hence the predicament of the fallen soul in the *Exegesis on the Soul*, who whores herself and is continually bearing deformed children), or even leave the infants out to die, the unpredictable results of which practice were dramatized in Sophocles' *Oedpius Rex*.

To Gnostics, sexuality had an additional dimension. Sex would result in pregnancy and childbirth, and another child would be brought into the world. The resulting baby would be a prison for a seed of light from the Pleroma. Would a Gnostic wish to trap a part of God in matter by having a child? This does seem to have been a genuine concern for some Gnostics, and celibacy was the simplest way to be certain of not imprisoning another soul in matter. But others probably reasoned that the spark of light would be able to escape again, join the Pleroma and be restored to divinity, and that the experience of the soul in this vale of tears might actually add to the quality of the Pleroma.

In the ancient world, celibacy was an accepted way of life for certain minority groups. They may have been mocked by the culture at large, but many pagan philosophers looked to celibacy as a way of liberating themselves from the desires of the body (meat was considered to enflame the passions, so a celibate philosopher would not wish to eat red meat each day), and heterodox Jewish groups such as the Essenes also promoted celibacy. Encratism is a form of asceticism that includes celibacy and vegetarianism. Irenaeus believed, or at least claimed in writing, that the Encratites were a separate sect that descended from Satornilos and Marcion.

Asceticism can indeed degenerate into a hatred of the world and a disgust at the flesh, and conventional Christians questioned the motives of Gnostic asceticism. If Gnostic asceticism was based on a rejection of this world, and of the demiurgic God that ruled it, then Christians could interpret this as a rejection of what is good in the world, since according to their own beliefs, the creator God was identical with the true and good God, who made the world good. They saw Gnostic (and Marcionite) asceticism as yet another Gnostic perversion. Yet ascetic practices followed Christianity through its various forms, and the monasticism that was founded in Egypt by St Anthony and became so popular there, and surely supplanted

Gnosticism in some places, was based on the most extreme forms of encratic asceticism. In their hagiographies we find desert fathers digging up the corpses of old girlfriends and hugging them in an effort to free themselves from the desires of the flesh. Now, if a Gnostic had done that, what fun the heresy-hunters would have had in condemning them and putting necrophiliac motives onto them.

Our knowledge of libertine Gnostic practices is on less firm ground than our knowledge of Gnostic asceticism. Gnostic libertine practices may be characterized as a variety of anti-nomianism, a term that literally means 'against the law'. Antinomianism is a spiritual practice that deliberately ignores or goes against contemporary mores or morality. It may be a belief that religious or civil law no longer applies to those who are spiritually developed, or it may be a technique that uses the intense experience of opposing the norms of society and religion to create a particular disinhibited psychological state.

There are antinomian tendencies in the very earliest Christians, and the Christian rejection of Jewish food laws and circumcision was initially a form of antinomianism. In the gospels Jesus is depicted as being very lax in his observance of Jewish law. He considers Sabbath observance to be less important than healing, and his disciples pluck corn on the Sabbath. Jesus was a Galilean, and the people of Galilee were well known for their sloppy attitude towards Torah observance. (Whether any of this really relates to a historical Jesus is of course another matter.) But strict Torah observance swiftly became an issue for Christians when Paul extended the branch of Christian salvation to non-Jews.

Paul felt that the message of Christ Crucified nullified the old law, or at least diminished its importance, and Gentile Christians were therefore not bound to keep Jewish traditions. As we have seen, Paul was an important figure for the Gnostics, particularly for Valentinians and the Marcionites. In his rejection of the law, Paul was speaking specifically about ritual purity, not about morality, and his morality was still very Jewish – his sexual morality in particular was very strict. Paul would in no way have approved of sexual libertinism. But the Pauline principle of the old law having passed away could be extended by some Gnostics into situations that had not been intended by Paul. Perhaps a strict sexual morality was only appropriate for psychics, for those who followed the outer meaning of the scriptures, the letter of the law.

Some Gnostic leaders, such as Carpocrates and Cerinthus were accused of being antinomian by the heresy-hunting Church Fathers, whose descriptions of antinomian Gnostic practices range from eating food offered to pagan idols to debauched orgies involving the consumption of bodily fluids. The most notorious of the libertine practices of the Gnostics are described in Epiphanius, who journeyed to Egypt in 335 CE at the age of 20. He somehow met up with a Gnostic group whom he thought were ordinary Christians, but he later called Stratiotics or Phibionites or Barbelites. He describes a sect who engaged in orgies, and then allegorized passages from the Bible to explain the importance of consuming semen and menstrual blood, which they themselves consumed at the peak of their rites. Epiphanius really twisted the knife when he alleged that in the event that a woman of the sect became pregnant, the foetus would be aborted, ground up with a mortar and pestle, seasoned with honey, pepper and spices, and then consumed as a Passover meal.

According to Epiphanius, Carpocrates:

> 'Taught his followers to perform every
> obscenity and every sinful act. And unless one
> proceeds through all of them, he said, and
> fulfils the will of all demons and angels, he
> cannot mount to the highest heaven or get by
> the principalities and authorities.'[31]

His description of the sect is horrendous, of course, but how true is it? Did Epiphanius, who later became the bishop of Salami, take part in these things? Can we imagine him with cupped hands, about to drink his own semen but thinking better of it and going off to consult a bishop instead? Or daintily passing on the pestle containing the abortion? Another extract from Epiphanius has him describing a further rite in which the Gnostics kiss a snake and then worship it. He quotes a lost *Gospel of Eve* as justifying these practices, and the late Gnostic text *Pistis Sophia* itself knew of similar rumours and condemned similar practices, showing that even if some Gnostics did practise these things, they were not typical.

But it was not only Gnostics who were accused of these extreme perversions. The second-century Christian apologist Minucius Felix describes some of the claims that pagan writers had made concerning ordinary Catholic Christians. Christians were accused of baking pies and inserting living babies into the pastry, which new converts to Christianity then sliced up with their knives and ate, reminiscent of the story of the Greek Thyestes who at a banquet was served his own son in a dish.

The pagan enemies of Minucius Felix also claimed that

Christians filled themselves with wine and food in a very similar way to Epiphanius' Gnostics. When the feast was finished they threw meat to a dog which was tied to the single lampstand providing light to the feast. The dog ran to get the meat, the lampstand toppled over, and the disgusting Christians used the resulting darkness for a no-holds-barred orgy. If we should trust Epiphanius on the Gnostics, perhaps we should also trust Minucius Felix's pagan source on the Christians, which is actually a couple of centuries earlier. These kinds of claims resurfaced periodically when Christians were launching attacks against heretics, and the Bogomils were accused of similar crimes.

Libertinism, if used intelligently and honestly for a limited period can lead to a breaking down of taboos, to free people from the devices that the archons use to keep the soul attached to the morality of this world. But as a regular practice libertinism is dangerous, and in a group context can easily corrupt.

* * *

References to repeated vowel sequences and bizarre, longwinded names whose meanings are difficult to discover are found in a number of Gnostic texts, in the inscriptions on the Gnostic magical gems and in the accounts of the heresiologists. These names are often related to the Hebrew name of God, YHWH, which was a secret name, written and transmitted without the vowels necessary to pronounce it. But in fact it is not the meaning of these words but their action that is important.

In the Hermetic Nag Hammadi text, *The Discourse on the Eighth and the Ninth*, we find a prayer that ends with a mysterious name bookending a sequence of vowels: 'Zoxathazo a oo ee ooo eee oooo ee oooooo ooooo oooooo uuuuuu oooooooooooo ooo Zozazoth.'

And in the *Gospel of the Egyptians*: 'iiiiiiiiiiiiiiiiiiiiii
EEEEEEEEEEEEEEEEEEEEEE oooooooooooooooooooooo uuuu
uuuuuuuuuuuuuuuuuu eeeeeeeeeeeeeeeeeeeeee aaaaaaaaaaaaaaa
aaaaaaa OOOOOOOOOOOOOOOOOOOOOO'.

These vowels (repeated 22 times each, perhaps for the 22
letters of the Hebrew alphabet) are linked to the audible name of
the Father. The Father himself is said to exist in silence, but
this repetition of vowels is his name 'in invisible symbol'. Similar
sequences of sounds exist in other texts like *Zostrianos*, in the
inscriptions on magical gems and in the magical papyri.

In Pythagorean tradition the sounds of the vowels reflected
the qualities of the seven classical planets. These are the seven
Greek vowels, alpha, eta (long E), epsilon (short E), iota, omicron
(short O), upsilon and omega (long O). They were probably used
in vocalized or internally recited repetitive techniques, a form of
spiritual praxis that exists in several traditions. In Tibetan
Buddhism, the mantra is well known; in Islam it is called the
dhikr or *zikhr*. In the Christian Orthodox tradition, prayers such
as the Lord's Prayer or the Jesus Prayer were recited internally
and continuously.

Such techniques can be used as exercises to develop attention
and repeated practice can lead to a state in which the prayer or
repetition may appear to continue by itself, and the part of the
person that is doing the prayer appears separate from an element
in the person that is watching it. Thus the technique forces an
internal division or separation that the Gnostics could have
understood as the experience of the spirit being present to the
soul's inner world. The key to exercises like these is recognizing
(*knowing*) the sense of separateness from oneself that develops
and not becoming too over-infatuated with other alluring aspects

of the experience. One may simply consider it to be a form of meditation, in which the meaninglessness of the sounds gives the mind something to focus on but gives it no associative material with which it might wander off.

In modern psychology, the recital or repetition of meaning-less phrases is recognized as leading to an unusual psychological state, called *jamais vu* (never seen). This is in distinction to *déjà vu*, the feeling that something has already been seen or has happened before. When Chris Moulin, a researcher at Leeds University, asked 92 volunteers to write out the word 'door' 30 times in 60 seconds, he found that 68 per cent of his guinea pigs 'showed symptoms of *jamais vu*, such as beginning to doubt that "door" was a real word.'[32]

As a child of about seven years, I started repeating my own name to myself until it became meaningless. Even my own identity came into question and was replaced by a different, vivid sense of 'I' and a feeling that lasted only briefly but left its trace, that it was only at that time that I knew my true identity and true purpose in the world.

So clearly the Gnostics discovered that this was an effective technique. It would also seem that these were not just mental exercises but were actually voiced aloud. The Neoplatonist Plotinus criticized Gnostics for their 'melodies', 'shrieks', 'whis-perings and hissings with the voice'.[33]

Aside from the repetitive disciplines, Gnostics had other forms of prayer, many of which are scattered throughout the surviving texts. The extant Gnostic codices do not contain only text: as well as the occasional *ankh* and other decorative glyphs, a few genuinely Gnostic diagrams have survived. There is also a description of the Ophite diagram, which can be reconstructed. The *Books of Jeu* in the Bruce Codex is heavily illustrated by diagrams: mysterious, often rather witchy-looking pictures that are intrinsic to the text and enable the often complex mythological systems and listings of spiritual levels and deities to be understood schematically. The Gnostics recognized that diagrams, like myths, can offer a non-verbal, or non-logical approach to a concept. In the *Books of Jeu*, visual signs and seals are assigned to the various aeons and archons in a very magical way.

The Ophite diagram is described in the refutation of Christianity and Gnosticism written by the second-century pagan Celsus. The text of Celsus has not itself survived, but extracts from it are contained in the Church Father Origen's own refutation of Celsus, *Contra Celsum*.[34] The diagrams that Celsus described and which Origen viewed are somewhat difficult to reconcile, and it is not clear whether they are the same diagrams, but they each encapsulate a Gnostic cosmology. Celsus' diagram had ten circles within a larger circle named 'Leviathan', with a line named Gehenna dividing the diagram into two. The diagram must have been complex, as Celsus described:

> 'They continue to heap together one thing after
> another – discourses of prophets, and circles upon
> circles, and effluents from an earthly church, and
> from circumcision; and a power flowing from one
> Prunicos, a virgin and a living soul; and a heaven
> slain in order to live, and an earth slaughtered by
> the sword, and many put to death that they may
> live, and death ceasing in the world, when the sin
> of the world is dead; and, again, a narrow way,
> and gates that open spontaneously.'

Origen's diagram had two concentric circles, a larger circle marked 'Father' and a smaller circle marked 'Son'.

> 'And between the greater circle (in which the lesser was contained) and another composed of two circles – the outer one of which was yellow, and the inner blue – a barrier inscribed in the shape of a hatchet. And above it, a short circle, close to the greater of the two former, having the inscription "Love"; and lower down, one touching the same circle, with the word "Life". And on the second circle, which was intertwined with and included two other circles, another figure, like a rhomboid, [entitled] "The foresight of wisdom". And within their point of common section was "The nature of wisdom". And above their point of common section was a circle, on which was inscribed "Knowledge"; and lower down another, on which was the inscription, "Understanding".'[35]

* * *

Ritual is as fundamental to religion as scripture is, and all religions have some sort of ritual practice. Sacramental ritual was important to all branches of Gnosticism. The Sethians focused particularly on a kind of baptism ritual.[36] In Sethian texts, there are many references to five seals, which may represent five stages of a Sethian baptism, five degrees of initiation. John Turner, the world's foremost expert in Sethianism, feels that Sethian rituals are both sacred actions and also representative of inner transformation.

'Terms that ordinarily refer to ritual acts, such as
"baptism", "immersion", "disrobing",
"enrobing", "stripping off", "putting on",
"sealing", and the like, also designate acts of
mental transformation, conceptual refinement and
abstraction from the world of psychic and
sensible experience, abstention from previous
behavioural dispositions, "unlearning" of older
and adoption of new perceptions of self and
world, and entrance into a higher state of enlightenment. It is natural to assume that such a mental
transformation arose out of the individual
experience of actual cultic and ritual praxis of a
sort that could be taught and enacted either while
participating in the physical setting and
associated gestures of the rite or quite apart from
them.'[37]

The Sethians had five seals of baptism, while the Valentinian
Gnostics practised five unrelated sacraments, which are
explicitly listed in the *Gospel of Philip* 60: 'The Lord did
everything in a mystery: a baptism and a chrism and a eucharist
and a redemption and a holy bridal chamber.' Later Gnostic or
Gnostic-related movements also had sacramental elements to
them. For the Bogomils and the Cathars, the rite of the consolamentum was central to salvation, for the Mandaeans it was
baptism too. In *The Gospel of Philip: Annotated & Explained*, I
addressed the Valentinian sacraments described in the gospel
allegorically and symbolically in connection with what I feel is
the overall hermeneutic of the *Gospel of Philip*.

Sacraments are not unique to Gnosticism of course and are perhaps even more fundamental to mainstream Christianity. The rites of baptism and the Eucharist or Mass, the taking of bread and wine, have inarguably been part of Christianity at least since the time of Paul, and they owe their rationale to events that are said to have happened in Jesus' lifetime.

Valentinianism invested so heavily in allegory and symbolism that we cannot be sure to what extent the sacraments were important in themselves, and not only for their inner meaning. With the redemption, for example, it is actually unclear whether this was practised as a rite or was entirely spiritual.

The Valentinians were said to practise a second (and a third) baptism in addition to the ordinary Christian baptism, and this higher baptism could sometimes be known as the redemption. According to the Gnostic Theodotus, once baptism and the attendant catechetical knowledge (as in the famous quotation, the knowledge of 'who we were, what we have become…') are given to the Gnostic, he or she is no longer ruled by malign fate or the restrictive powers of astrology. Thus baptism represented the beginning of freedom and gnosis. According to one Gnostic view (preserved by Irenaeus), baptism for psychics was brought by John the Baptist, but baptism for pneumatics was brought by Christ, perhaps an echo of the story of Apollos in the Acts of the Apostles, who only knew of the baptism of John before he met Paul (Acts 18:24–19:7).

In the Valentinian texts there is a strange scheme of equivalence between the sacraments: baptism *is* redemption *is* the bridal chamber. Perhaps these mean that the inner pneumatic experience bequeathed by each of these rites is identical.

The rite of baptism covers a wide range of actual practices.

Gnostics held baptisms, as did Christians, and it was also a feature of first-century Jewish practice, hence the sect of John the Baptist. For the Essenes, baptismal and other water rites were also important. Baptism was particularly important to the Mandaeans as well (see Chapter 10), for whom it was more than a single initiatory episode, but a weekly sacrament and communion. Indeed, at least four of the five Valentinian sacraments correspond with basic human activities – washing, eating, sexual relationships, and (if redemption may be considered a funeral rite, as it sometimes is) death or funerary practices.

Whether the baptismal recipient was washed in a bath or cistern or in a river, baptism always involved water that was symbolically 'living'. Living water was probably synonymous with running water in early baptismal rites, but in Gnosticism it takes on a more symbolic meaning. In the *Gospel of Philip*, baptism is treated allegorically, though scholars have strained to extract actual practices from the spiritualized descriptions in Philip.

Others, again, lead them to a place where water is, and baptize them, with the utterance of these words:

> 'Into the name of the unknown Father of the
> universe – into truth, the mother of all things –
> into Him who descended on Jesus – into union,
> and redemption, and communion with the
> powers.'[38]

The rite of chrism or anointing was a simple one. Anointing with oil (usually olive oil) was a common practice in ancient Mediterranean religion, though it may seem a little exotic to northern peoples. Bread, water, wine and oil, fruit and then fish too and perhaps a little meat, were essential ingredients of the Mediterranean diet. Anointing was an ancient Jewish practice, which consisted simply of olive oil being daubed on the forehead or other part of the head. Christians often received it in the form of the cross, and Gnostics too, if they did not find this reference to Jesus' literal physical crucifixion repugnant. The *Gospel of Philip* cleverly links the olive tree to the tree from which the cross was made, and hence 'From the olive tree comes chrism and from chrism the resurrection' (*Gospel of Philip* 80).

The symbolism of anointing was itself associated with messiah-hood. When Saul was made king of the Hebrews, he was anointed with oil by the priest Samuel, and was afterwards referred to as God's anointed. In Hebrew, the root word is *mashach* – anoint – which becomes *Christos* in Greek and Coptic. In English we use loan words from both Hebrew ('messiah') and Greek ('Christ'). The literal translation of this into English captures the sense well enough – the chrism makes a Christ of us. In the *Gospel of Philip* 83 it is said: 'Christ is lord over baptism. For it is from chrism that we are called Christians, not because of the baptism. And he was called Christ because of the chrism.'

Someone who has fulfilled the conditions of Gnosis 'is no longer a Christian, but a Christ'. (*Gospel of Philip* 59) The chrism was thought by the author or compiler of the *Gospel of Philip* to be more important than the baptism.

The Eucharist was probably practised by Valentinians in the same way as it was by Catholic Christians, but it was accompanied by a spiritual interpretation. The *Gospel of Philip* 24 does say that, 'He says today in the Eucharist, "You who have united the perfect light with the holy spirit, unite also our angels with the images."'

This may possibly be a fragment of a specifically Valentinian Eucharist. Nag Hammadi Codex XI 2 also contains a fragmentary text of a specifically Valentinian Eucharist. A second-century Eucharist was likely to be less formal than the forms of Eucharist practised in modern Churches, at least in 'High Church' traditions such as the Roman Catholic or Anglican. Among the *Gospel of Philip*'s other comments on the Eucharist is a simple statement of equivalence, 'The Eucharist is Jesus' (*Gospel of Philip* 46).

Another variety of Eucharist is described by Irenaeus in his polemical account of the Valentinian Markus. Irenaeus describes a Valentinian initiation ritual conducted by Markus, and in his typically hostile way he writes of a poor woman being made hysterical by the rite, and presents it as a clever conjuring trick by which a larger cup is filled with wine by a smaller cup so that the larger cup unexpectedly overflows. Irenaeus seems to think that this should terrify any poor neophyte who undergoes the initiation, but being in the role of an initiate during such an important ceremony would give one a heightened sense of awareness. As, against all expectations, the leader of the ritual continued to pour when the cup was already full, and the red wine flowed over the lip of the cup and onto the floor, the initiate would have been vividly aware of the present moment.

This highlights an important role of sacraments. A sacrament might be considered holy in itself, and in the Catholic Church, Christ is considered to have instituted the sacraments as a method in which he could 'communicate his grace'.[39] The sacraments are 'signs and instruments' by which Jesus' grace is spread. In a practical, spiritual sense, a sacrament may make one more aware of the present, of the holiness of life, and at the same time is a ritual expression of eternal truths and understanding that is put into actions rather than into words.

The rite of the bridal chamber may obviously be considered as a source of libertine practice. Irenaeus thought so:

> 'For some of them prepare a nuptial couch, and
> perform a sort of mystic rite (pronouncing certain
> expressions) with those who are being initiated,
> and affirm that it is a spiritual marriage which is
> celebrated by them, after the likeness of the con-
> junctions above.'[40]

But once again it is likely that the true bridal chamber was internal, the marriage of the soul and the spirit. Another situation in which the rite of the bridal chamber might take place is – a no-brainer, this one – after a wedding. The earthly, physical bonding of man and wife could be used to represent and remind the Gnostic of the union of spirit and soul that is at the heart of Gnosis.

* * *

The most mysterious and obscure of the Valentinian rites was the rite of redemption or apolytrosis. It was mysterious to Irenaeus too and he complained that 'there are as many schemes of "redemption" as there are teachers of these mystical opinions.'[41] And the rite of redemption certainly was the most fluid and least clearly defined (at least in our surviving literature) of all the Gnostic rites. It is sometimes claimed that the redemption was a second baptism; sometimes it is described as a kind of funeral rite. However, when Irenaeus describes these redemption rites he is actually detailing rites of chrism and baptism. Some Gnostics

rightly consider the redemption to be gnosis itself, not some
mere external rite, and they:

> 'Hold that the knowledge [*gnosis*] of the unspeak-
> able Greatness is itself perfect redemption. For
> since both defect and passion flowed from
> ignorance, the whole substance of what was thus
> formed is destroyed by knowledge [*gnosis*]; and
> therefore knowledge is the redemption of the
> inner man. This, however, is not of a corporeal
> nature, for the body is corruptible; nor is it
> animal, since the animal soul is the fruit of a
> defect, and is, as it were, the abode of the spirit.
> The redemption must therefore be of a spiritual
> nature; for they affirm that the inner and spiritual
> man is redeemed by means of knowledge, and
> that they, having acquired the knowledge of all
> things, stand thenceforth in need of nothing else.
> This, then, is the true redemption.'[42]

Perhaps redemption was originally a sacrament with no rite, the
ultimate sacrament of gnosis in everyday life.

* * *

Magic was of course not a uniquely Gnostic practice, but magical
practices are present in Gnostic texts. Ancient magic was a form
of popular religion, and an extensive number of spells, written
on papyrus, have survived. These cover the usual range of folk
magic, from healing and medicinal spells to love potions to
money-making spells and curses. The full range of pagan gods,
from Greek, Egyptian and near Eastern pantheons, is invoked,
and it is this syncretistic ancient pagan magical tradition that was

picked up in the occult revival and formulated by such modern Western occultists as Aleister Crowley.

The ancient magical tradition appealed for aid from any god who might be appropriate to the magic being worked. Hence there are many spells, preserved in Coptic and Greek, that invoke Jesus, or Mary, or the Christian God or the Jewish God. The Jewish God, with his mysterious vowelless unpronounceable name had a particular appeal because the naming of a god was a prime magical activity. Marvin Meyer has published a selection of Egyptian Christian magical papyri in Coptic,[43] and the overall impression is very different to anything we have been brought up to expect in early Christianity. Therefore it is no surprise that we also find distinctly Gnostic names, like Abraxas or IAO or Ialdabaoth in some of the papyri, along with the vowel sequences that have been mentioned above. In addition to the papyri, many Greco-Egyptian magical gems survive. These are often called Gnostic gems, but it is only those with distinctively Gnostic names and depictions that can be truly categorized as Gnostic. The best of the gems have an arcane beauty to them, and to see them and realize that they were once held warm in the hands of Gnostic Copts brings an immediacy to the study of the ancient Gnostics.

The Valentinian teacher Markus, whose wine ritual was described above, has often been nicknamed Markus the Magician, and Irenaeus attributed a number of magical rites to him. We might quite reasonably include the naming of the archons and the 'passwords' given to them during the ascent of the soul as a form of 'magic'. But the working of magic would be beside the point to the most pneumatic Gnostics. The aim of healing magic is to affect the material world – the world of matter or the body. The aim of curses or love spells or magic that attracts wealth is similarly to influence the material world, or at best the world of the soul, the world of earthly emotions. Thus magic was concerned only with the psychic and hylic/choic worlds. Why would a true Gnostic wish to ask favours of the demiurge, a demiurge that created this world out of ignorance and knows nothing of the higher world of the Pleroma?

In fact, the Gnostic view could be actually hostile to magic for the above reasons. In the *Pistis Sophia*, Mary asks Jesus whether the magic of the 'astrologers' and 'soothsayers' will continue to work now that Jesus has come. Jesus had said that he took away a third of the power of the archons and turned around the sphere that the archons rule. Jesus replies that their 'evil magic' and astrology will no longer work now that he has reduced the power of the archons.[44]

Astrology is often seen as an 'evil magic' because it belongs to Heimarmene, Fate. The archons use the influence of the planets and stars to bind humans to their fate, to predetermine their actions, bind them to the material world and keep them recognizing the Pleroma. Other Gnostics did practise astrology and magic. We know that Mandaean priests practised astrology to an extensive degree, despite the influence of the stars and the planets being denigrated in their myths.

Thus the Gnostics had many practices and rituals, but these were secondary to gnosis. In the confusion of the sequence and hierarchy of the Valentinian sacraments, and the interpretation of each sacrament as illustrating a variety of gnosis, we can even see that what is distinctive about Gnostics is always gnosis, not praxis.

CHAPTER 6

THE BIRTH OF GNOSTICISM

'Until baptism, they say, Fate is real, but after it the astrologists are no longer right. But it is not only the washing that is liberating, but the knowledge of who we were, and what we have become, where we were or where we were placed, whither we hasten, from what we are redeemed, what birth is and what rebirth.'

THEODOTUS[45]

The Gnostics were clear about their origins: they knew who they were and what they had become, where they were or where they were placed. They came from the Pleroma, the level of reality that is directly connected to the true and highest God, who is a unity, who is the Father. And it is to the Pleroma that they will return. Even within their earthly lives Gnostics could regain their connection to the Pleroma and re-experience it.

The Gnostics spent much time clarifying the meaning of the book of Genesis, but unfortunately for us, they were not quite so

clear about their historical genesis. We are left with the Gnostics'
mythical accounts of their own origins, with the polemics of
the Church Fathers, and with a great deal of suggestive material
and inferences with which a historical mosaic might be created.
Tied in with the issue of origins is the question of whether the
Gnostics were Christian heretics or not.

The Sethian Gnostics are so named because they considered
themselves to belong to the generation of Seth, or seed of Seth,
who occupies only a few small verses in Genesis chapters 4 and
5, in which we learn only that he was the third son of Adam and
Eve, that he was father to Enosh – also an important mystical
figure in some traditions – and that he lived to the age of
800–900 years or so. Seth represented a fresh beginning after the
tragedy of Cain and Abel, a new man who was neither murderer
nor victim. So the Sethians were mythologically descendants of
Seth, but this obviously gives us no direct historical data.

The Valentinians may have preferred to call themselves
Christians or pneumatics rather than Valentinians, but their
name at least directs us to their presumed point of origin. The
beginning of the Valentinians can clearly be traced back to
Valentinus himself. As to where Valentinus came from, and how
his teachings developed, we will encounter some conflicting
views. Valentinus came from Egypt, as did many of the earlier
Gnostics or proto-Gnostics, some of whom could easily have
been a direct influence on him.

It is once again to the writings of the Church Fathers that
we must turn in our search for the earliest Gnostics. The earliest
Gnostic teachers include Menander, Satornilos (or Saturninus
in the Latin), Basilides and Carpocrates, and the very earliest
Gnostic has a startlingly familiar name – Simon Magus. Simon

was the infamous figure from the Acts of the Apostles who was converted by Philip the evangelist and then offered to pay Peter and John so that he could receive the secrets of Jesus' teaching and the laying on of hands, thus giving rise to the term simony, the crime of paying for the privilege of ecclesiastical office.

Simon is often claimed as the earliest Gnostic, but it is difficult to determine how much of this might truly be historical and how much is merely the Church Fathers trying to blame the origin of Gnosticism on a notoriously dubious character from Acts. That is, was Simon Magus really a first-century Gnostic whose character was being tarnished in the proto-orthodox whitewashing of Acts, or was the tarnished character of Simon Magus pressed into service later as a justification for treating Gnosticism as a Christian heresy? Simon himself was the source of much later legend, particularly the story in the apocryphal Acts of Peter in which he flies up into the air in the marketplace in order to demonstrate his godlike abilities, but is brought down by the apostle Peter. Simon breaks his legs in falling and is stoned to death by the crowd.

In medieval legend, Simon developed into the archetypal heretic, and these stories were known throughout medieval Christendom. In Irish tradition Simon Magus was the teacher of a druid named Mug Ruith, who learnt the secrets of flight from Simon and built a wooden flying machine! According to Hippolytus, however, Simon died not as a Christian Icarus but had himself buried in preparation for his resurrection. According to the tale, he unfortunately wasn't resurrected, but suffocated to death in his grave.

According to Justin Martyr, who came from Samaria, Simon

Magus was himself a Samaritan. Samaria was perceived by Jews as a hotbed of heresy. It was actually nearer to Jerusalem than Galilee was, but it maintained quite separate traditions and in contrast to Galilee had not been recolonized by Judeans. The Samarian religion was based on the five books of the Torah, and the Samaritans still see themselves as the remains of the Israelite tribes of Ephraim and Manasseh, who survived the eighth-century destruction of the Northern kingdom by the Assyrians.[46] Simon was said to have been active in Samaria during the reign of Claudius (41–54 CE) which fits with his meeting with Peter and John in Acts. Simon claimed to be the 'power of God which is called "great"', according to Acts.

A text entitled *The Great Exposition* is probably from the second century, and whether or not Simon Magus was truly a Gnostic or proto-Gnostic, he was certainly seen as a mythical founder figure by later Gnostic groups. One fascinating legend that is told of him is obviously a variant of the story of the fallen soul that is redeemed, as in the *Exegesis on the Soul*. According to Justin Martyr and Irenaeus, Simon's female companion was a woman called Helena, who was named Ennoia or 'First Thought' by Simon. He found Helena, in Tyre, working as a prostitute, and he purchased her freedom from the brothel when he realized that she was the mother of all incarnated in human form. She had suffered a fall from grace, much as the soul in the *Exegesis on the Soul* had, and had been incarnated in many female bodies before she met Simon. One of these was the earlier Helena, Helen of Troy, and the appearance of Helen of Troy in the various versions of the Faust story can be traced back to Helena's association with Simon Magus. Simon acted as a redeemer figure, and grandiose claims were made of his importance to the world.

Just as with Jesus, Simon Magus has a torturous history, moving from historicity (though some would say that neither of them began as historical characters but as mythical creations) to legend and myth. Simon Magus became the archetypal heretic, a figure of inspiration or revulsion depending on one's point of view, and the legends of Simon fertilized many further stories.

As well as Faust's connection to Simon Magus, Shakespeare's play *Pericles Prince of Tyre*, a tale of redemption involving a prostitute in a brothel in Tyre, may also have drawn on the Simon Magus tradition.

Was Simon Magus truly an early Gnostic or proto-Gnostic? Or, was he just a charismatic Samaritan teacher who found himself on the wrong side of the emerging Christianity, if he existed at all? In the later Clementine literature, Simon Magus was a cipher for Paul.

To whatever extent the legend of Simon Magus may have been embroidered, there may be a historic core to it. Justin Martyr wrote that Simon Magus was the teacher of Menander, another early Gnostic of whom we know little save that he was also a Samaritan, who later moved to Antioch where he was accused of practising magic. His teaching also reflects a dualism between a primary power and the angels who created this world. According to Irenaeus, baptism into Menander's teaching was enough to give the initiate a spiritual resurrection.

Satornilos was seen as being in the same line. He was a pupil of Menander and a native of Antioch in Syria, and his teaching added to Menander's cosmology the influence of the seven angels, one of whom was the God of the Jews. Many familiar features of Gnosticism are apparent in Irenaeus' description of Satornilos' teaching.

The teaching of Basilides, who lived in Alexandria, seems to be somewhat closer to the Valentinian teaching, with Hermetic elements too, such as the Nous and Logos, and it is possible that Valentinus may have been a disciple of Basilides, in addition to Theudas who was a disciple of Paul. Basilides was said to have written his own gospel, plus a 24-book commentary on the canonical gospels, and hymns. Basilides himself was said to have been taught by Matthias, the apostle, who replaced Judas among the Twelve, and also to have been a disciple of Glaucias, a disciple of St Peter. Basilides' own son Isadore continued his teaching.

Thus we ostensibly have a neat lineage of Gnosticism as a Christian heresy, going on the one hand from Simon Magus, who knew Philip, Peter and John, to Menander then to Satornilos; and on the other hand from Peter to Glaucius, or from Matthias, to Basilides, then on perhaps to Valentinus. Irenaeus insisted on an alternative version that derived from Valentinus' lineage from Simon Magus rather than Paul. There are all sorts of problems in this appealing but simplistic genealogy of so-called heretics, but it at least points us in the right direction.

We can probably reject a single simplistic point of origin for the Gnostics. There was no single monolithic Gnostic Church, no single redeemer figure, and no single time or place at which Gnosticism hatched fully-formed out of its egg. It seems to have emerged spontaneously in a variety of places in the first and second centuries. The seed was the Platonic tradition, but the soil was the recently Hellenized countries of Egypt, Syria, Samaria and Palestine. But once the Gnostic world-view had appeared, once its meme had been sown into the world, it was here to stay.

In the ancient world, the division between town or city and country was pronounced. The artificiality of city life would seem more conducive to the development of Gnosticism than the more natural life of the countryside. Farmers and peasants, particularly in the ancient world, could suffer terrible conditions of life, but a dependency on the gods of the natural world, however quixotic their decisions and however unfair their treatment of humanity, does not lead to Gnostic dualism. Nature is unfair, but does not seem *wrong*.

Life in a city, however, can lead one to think that there is something fundamentally wrong with life and with the universe itself. Cities harbour and develop the highest and lowest aspects of civilization – indeed, the word civilization itself derives from the Latin *cives,* meaning city. Existential angst and philosophical speculation thrive in town, not country, as does the rejection of traditional religion. The particular city in which Gnosticism most likely developed was Alexandria.

The modern Egyptian Coptic Church now claims Mark the evangelist as its founder and prides itself on its orthodoxy, but this is unlikely, and Christianity probably came to Egypt in a variety of forms. Christianity was possibly not perceived as separate from its parent, Judaism, until the Jewish revolt under Trajan, between 115 and 117 CE. Carpocrates, Epiphanes (Carpocrates' son), Basilides and Valentinus are all said to be Egyptian. Alexandria had a large Jewish quarter occupying two-fifths of the city and had a Jewish Temple of its own at Leontopolis. The Leontopolis Temple is now little known, but at the time presented an alternative to the Jerusalem Temple for Egyptian Jews. It was built in the middle of the second century BCE and worship at the temple was terminated by Rome in 74 CE, shortly after the destruction of the Jerusalem Temple. While it was active, sacrifices were made in Leontopolis, and Jewish ritual purity could be renewed in accordance with Torah law. Many other Egyptian cities had large Jewish populations too, but Alexandria was in every respect an extraordinary city:

> 'Within a century after Alexandria was built, it was larger than Carthage and growing so swiftly that it acknowledged no superior, even Rome. It had already become the centre not only of Hellenism, but also of Judaism. Its Mouseion was the leading university of its time – the finest teachers, philosophers, and scientists flourishing within its walls. Here ancient scholars produced the Septuagint (Greek translation of the Hebrew Old Testament), and on these streets Julius Caesar would stroll with Cleopatra to the wild cheers of the populace.'[47]

There were three main districts: the Greek, the Egyptian and the Jewish, divided by the two great 30m/100ft-wide avenues of the Canopic Way and the Street of the Soma. The Jewish city was governed by its own ethnarch and a council, and was only slightly smaller than the Greek quarter. According to the first-century Jewish historian Josephus, Jews had lived alongside Greeks in their respective quarters of the city since shortly after the death of Alexander the Great. Alexandrian Jews were often wealthy and well educated in Greek culture as well as in their own traditions.

C.G. Jung called Alexandria the city where East meets West. Alexandria was the inheritor of the ancient Egyptian tradition, the Hellenistic Greek tradition and the Jewish tradition. The Egyptian tradition had been Hellenized and fed into the syncretistic pagan religion that covered the ancient Hellenistic world. Gods from different traditions were absorbed into the general mass of religion, and figures from diverse traditions, such as Serapis, Cybele and Isis, were worshipped throughout the Eastern empire. Judaism itself was Hellenized, and Alexandrian Jews spoke Greek and read the Old Testament in the Greek language. Figures such as Philo of Alexandria adapted the Jewish traditions to Greek philosophy using the allegorical method. However, despite this apparent harmony, Jews and Greeks did not always live peacefully in Alexandria, and Jews were subject to periodic bouts of persecution and their right to apply their own laws was continually being eroded.

Historical calamities are yet other factors that might have led to the emergence of the Gnostic viewpoint. The disastrous Jewish revolts and wars with the Romans led to the Jewish diaspora, a significant downturn in Jewish status in the Roman Empire, and a massive change in Jewish religious practices. In 70 CE the Jerusalem Temple was destroyed during the first Jewish War, and between 115 and 117 CE another Jewish revolt occurred in Egypt. In the Second Jewish War (132–35 CE), the Bar Kokhba revolt, Jerusalem itself was razed and replaced with a Roman-style city named Aelia Capitolina.

Despite, or perhaps because of, the political and social turbulence in Jewish society, it was an astonishingly fertile time. Christianity, Gnosticism and rabbinical Judaism are all fruits of this period. Edmondo Lupieri, an Italian scholar of Gnosticism, has pointed out that the second and third centuries were an incredibly fertile time in Egypt, comparable in their religious fecundity only to sixteenth-century Reformation Europe and California in the 1960s and 1970s – about 70 new Christian denominations were formed every day at the end of the 1960s.

* * *

All of the above are historical factors that may have contributed to the Gnostic outlook, along with the existence of non-main-stream forms of Hellenistic Judaism, and a turbulence in society that would have caused people to doubt the omnipotence or the justice of their monotheistic God. There was massive disruption and wholesale slaughter, deportation and exile, and the Jerusalem Temple, the centre of Judaism, was destroyed. It was no wonder that the emerging Gnostics would have questioned the God of this world. But alongside this there was a great awakening, spiritu-ally, culturally and morally. In many ways the first and second centuries were not unlike our own times.

It is quite possible that Gnostic or proto-Gnostic ideas also emerged spontaneously in Syria or Palestine, where Judaism also met Hellenistic culture. Perhaps the time had come for Gnosticism. There were also predecessors to the Gnostics in the Hellenistic mystery religions (and the category of mystery religion is one in which we might include some of the Gnostic groups and even Christianity itself), in the dualism of the Zoroastrian religion, or parallel developments in writings of the Hermetists.

The Hermetica is a body of work ascribed to the legendary Hermes Trismegistus and his pupils. The Hermetica were written in the first three centuries CE, in Greek, probably in Alexandria. They are Platonic in inspiration and form, but also contain material related to the Egyptian tradition, and the philosophy is not entirely consistent throughout the material. In some of the

Hermetic writings we find a demiurge, a second God who is a son of God and who is the creator of this world. But the demiurge of the Hermetica is neither evil nor ignorant, and has been derived directly from Platonism without the startling transformation of the Gnostic demiurge.

The figure of Hermes Trismegistus came about through a transformation and adaptation of Thoth, the Egyptian god of wisdom, into his Greek counterpart Hermes. Trismegistus means 'thrice great' and is an epithet of Thoth that has been transferred to Hermes. In some of the Hermetica, Hermes teaches his pupils, Tat or Asklepius; in others, Hermes himself is the student, not the instructor, or Tat and Asklepius themselves instruct kings in the Hermetic mysteries.

When the Hermetic literature made its entry into Western European society in the early Renaissance, the scholars presumed wrongly (based on the account of Hermes Trismegistus by the third-century Church Father Lactianus) that Hermes was a historical individual who preceded Plato and was even a contemporary of Moses.

The strands of connection between the Gnostics and the Hermetica are complex and unresolved. Sethian and Valentinian Gnostic writings always exhibit Christian or Jewish features. The Hermetica may occasionally display a slight familiarity with Jewish ideas, but these are small exceptions to the pagan base and framework of the Hermetica. The Hermetica may be called a kind of pagan Gnosticism. The Hermetica is also syncretistic, combining elements of Platonism with Greco-Egyptian religion, and even a smidgen of Judaism. There is even less historical evidence for the conception and background of the Hermetica than there is for the Gnostics.

Unlike the Neoplatonists, there is no record of ancient Hermetists interacting with Gnostics. But we do know that the Gnostics appreciated Hermetic material (or at least that whoever put together Codex VI of the Nag Hammadi Library felt that Hermetic texts were not out of place alongside Gnostic and other esoteric Christian material) because the Nag Hammadi Library contains some Hermetica: *The Discourse on the Eighth and Ninth*, the *Prayer on Thanksgiving* and a large portion of Asklepius.

The Hermetists were themselves inspired by developments in Platonism in Alexandria. I cannot do better than quote a paragraph from Gilles Quispel, written as a preface to *The Way of Hermes*:

> 'In the century before Christ, the influential Stoic
> philosopher Posidonius taught that the cosmos
> was dominated by the "sympathy of all things"
> (stars and events on earth), that God was a Spirit,
> which pervaded the All, and that man was con-
> substantial with God, because he had a Spirit. At
> the same time a certain Eudorus, a Platonist, was
> teaching in Alexandria, stressing the religious
> elements, like reincarnation, in Plato and trying
> to reconcile Plato with Aristotle. The Hermetists
> followed these figures in using philosophic
> languages to express fundamentally religious
> teachings.'[48]

Like the writings of the Gnostics, Hermetic writings originated in Alexandria as a result of Platonist thought meeting religious thought. As with the Gnostics, the combining of more than one element led to a transformation. Hermetism was a new teaching, not merely a blending of Platonism and paganism. Myth and dialogue were as important to the Hermetists as to the Gnostics, though the Hermetic dialogues did not usually focus on oral sayings per se, rather on the discourse between teacher and pupil, often not systematically presented.

The Hermetic material is not very consistent in its philosophy, but we have already mentioned that this is something that Hermetism has in common with the Gnostics. The demiurgic creator is good, made in the image of the ultimate God, and his goodness may be present everywhere in the world, but there is evil also, and man particularly has an evil strain. Gnosis of the Supreme Good has been proclaimed, but many do not listen. Those who listen to the call may 'seek one who will lead you by the hand to the gates of the knowledge in your heart.'[49]

It is the heart's gnosis and the spiritual Nous that can guide mankind. Ignorance, evil, darkness, living death, the robber within one's own house, are all aspects of what keeps us from gnosis of the Nous – the body or the false self prevent us from being in contact with Nous. Gnosis often plays a part in the Hermetica, but it is the Nous, the concept of divine Mind, that occupies the pivotal place in the Hermetic literature.

In the *Poimandres*, the first text in the Corpus Hermeticum, the mythical personages are familiar. There is the Anthropos, the primal or ideal Man, who was initially both male and female; there are the planetary governors that are connected with Fate (Heimarmene) and the malign astrological influences that are associated with the soul and that have to be negotiated in the ascent of the soul. God the Father, the Word (Logos), a hymn to the Supreme God, are all contained there, and the text hints at a knowledge of the Book of Genesis. But there are no Christian elements in the Hermetica.

What survives is the Corpus Hermeticum (the rediscovery of which, at the beginning of the European Renaissance, was to have a huge influence): the three texts from Codex VI of the NHL, along with a Latin translation of *Asklepios*, *The Definitions of Hermet Trismegistus to Asklepios*, the anthology of Ioannes Stobaios, and references in magical literature. The confusingly named technical Hermetica – as opposed to the philosophical Hermetica, which consist of the texts mentioned above – comprise magical and astrological texts that are attributed to Hermes Trismegistus or invoke his name in some way. The oldest of these technical Hermetica dates to the first century.

We are on firm ground in looking at the Gnostics as having developed in the fertile intellectual soil of Alexandrian Egypt, with Judaism and Platonism as father and mother. But we should also offer a nod to similarly early origins in Syria and Palestine, whether the Gnosticism in these countries arose as a spontaneous parallel development or whether it also owes its ultimate origins to Egyptian Platonic speculation.

The ancient Gnostics were relatively short-lived in comparison to Christianity. By the end of the fourth century they were facing serious opposition, and though some remnants of the second-century Gnostic groups staggered on in isolation for a few more centuries, the Sethians and Valentinians were in terminal decline. It was not Constantine the Great, the first Christian Roman emperor, who ultimately forced out heterodox Christian groups, but his successor Theodosius. During his reign extensive anti-heretical legislation was passed, many non-orthodox sects, including the Valentinians and Marcionites, were persecuted and the private houses in which they met were confiscated by the state. The Gnostics were on the way to disappearing for good, but Gnosticism itself would continue.

Once ideas have been introduced into the world, they have their own existence, waiting for human heads and hearts to pick them up and make use of them again. Despite the enforced decline of the ancient Gnostics, their view of the world – in which a lower God is responsible for the catastrophe of most civilization, while a true God waits, unknown, to be discovered by personal gnosis – would survive.

We can see a direct historical lineage that stretches from the ancient Gnostics to the Manichaeans, then on to the Paulicians and Bogomils until it culminates in the Cathars, where it is once again destroyed by the forces of ignorant demiurgic religion. But the ideas also took root in other places, or emerged spontaneously in other cultures. Even the rediscovery of ancient Gnostic texts could be enough to reignite the eternal flame. You, after all, are reading this book.

CHAPTER 7

LIGHT AND DARKNESS: THE MANICHAEANS

Perhaps it was in the nature of the ancient Gnostics – the Valentinians, Sethians and others – to fade away so rapidly and to remain minority groups. Although there are reports of Valentinians surviving up to the eighth century, the classical Gnostics diminished in numbers and influence from the fourth century. Gradually, texts were no longer copied, Valentinians were no longer present at church services, or interpreting the gospel teachings esoterically and offering a higher level of spiritual (pneumatic) experience than the conventional religion of mere psychic Christians.

It was perhaps the very lack of dogma and the low degree of organization and political power in Gnostic groups that prevented them from spreading widely and becoming a large-scale religion. Marcionism, Gnosticism without gnosis, thrived as a religion but eventually lost out to mainstream Christianity. As a result, Gnostic teachings have perennially been perceived as heretical versions of mainstream Christianity, or sometimes of other religions. The ancient Gnostics, the Cathars and the

Bogomils were all considered by Christians to be Christian heresies – that is, they were thought to have originated in mainstream Christianity but had perverted the teaching of Christ and the Church, whether by their own misunderstandings or through the devil's influence.

Even the single branch of Gnostic teaching that truly became a religion on a larger scale, even a world religion, was claimed by Christians as a heresy of their own religion. This was Manichaeanism, the religion of light, a dualist religion with a mythology that is immediately reminiscent of older Gnostic mythologies. Evidence of Manichaeanism exists as far west as Spain and as far east as China, from the third century to, if only in the vaguest traces, the twenty-first.

Manichaeanism developed in Syria and spread principally eastward, but it was not limited to the Near East, and Manichaeans became the bugbears of medieval Western Christianity. Even more than the term 'Gnostic', 'Manichaean' became synonymous with world-hating dualism. More recently it has come to refer to any extreme black-and-white viewpoint, and US president George Bush Jr has been accused of having a Manichaean vision since the 9/11 attacks. One cannot imagine that the peace-loving and spiritual Manichaeans would have been pleased with the comparison.

Manichaeanism was named after its third-century founder, Mani. It is quite easy to put together a short biography of Mani's life, but it should be remembered that much of the source material is legendary, mythical or hagiographical. This is a problem for writers of history but a pleasure for lovers of esoteric scripture. For instance, Mani was contacted by his divine twin or light-self when he was aged 12. This was surely inspired by

Luke's story of Jesus in the Temple at the same age (12 being a significant number in many ancient traditions).

Mani was born on 14 April 216 CE near the Persian capital city Seleucia-Ctesiphon. His mother, Maryam or Mary (which name may be authentic, but again suggests that the story may be fashioned somewhat after the childhood story of Jesus), was said to have belonged to the imperial family, and his father, Pattak, also seemed to have been of noble birth. His father joined a baptizing sect called the Elkasaites, who were heterodox, but not Gnostic, and seem to have appeared around 100 CE in Syria. They were Christians who claimed as their founder Elkesai ('the hidden power of God').

The Elkasaites may have been related to the Mandaeans, or it is also possible that Mani may have had separate contact with Mandaeans. Mani saw himself as a religious leader, and, in accordance with the revelations granted to him by his divine twin, tried to reform the Elkasaite sect in which he grew up. This led to a schism within the sect and he was expelled from the group, with only three disciples following him, one of whom was his father.

It was, suspiciously, at the age of 24 (12 + 12), on 19 April 240 CE, that he received his call to be the 'apostle of light'. Following this, he established the first Manichaean community in Seleucia-Ctesiphon. He taught and gathered converts in Iran, then sent missionaries to the west, which in this context means the eastern Roman Empire, while he himself travelled to India and converted the ruler of Turan. Thus, in geographical terms, the spread of Manichaeanism easily exceeded the early spread of Christianity within a similar period.

After a couple of years of travelling he returned to Babylonia, where Shapur I had become king. He was well received in this kingdom and two of the king's brothers became followers. The dualistic nature of Mani's religion fitted easily into a country used to dualistic Zoroastrianism, which was surely a source of and influence on Mani's thought, and he acknowledged Zoroaster as a prophet and saviour. Mani's religion was syncretistic or eclectic in that it combined sources from several other traditions, but it added them to a basic worldview and a complex myth that was his own.

Mani's dualism had much in common with the Persian tradition, but his Gnosticism was probably derived from Syriac traditions, such as Eastern Valentinianism, Thomasine Christianity and the Gnostic Bardesanes. Little is known of the Elkaisite communities and teaching, but Mani may well have inherited some inklings of the Gnostic outlook from the community in which he grew up.

Mani's biography presents his initial spiritual experience (his meeting with his twin) and his decision to teach his revelations, but he may have spontaneously awakened and reinterpreted the traditions with which he was familiar. History can follow only the chain of tradition and describe the claims a teacher ('apostle' in the terminology of the Manichaeans) makes about himself, but can indicate nothing of the genuineness of an experience or the validity of an interpretation.

After Shapur I died, Ohrmuzd I was briefly king of Babylon, and he too was sympathetic to Mani. Mani continued to travel widely on missionary journeys, and it seems that he was intentionally trying to develop and promulgate a brand new religion. He established a canon of seven of his own writings, all of which were in Aramaic and none of which survives. Their evocative titles were *The Living Gospel*, *The Treasure of Life*, *The Pragmateia*, *The Book of Mysteries*, *The Book of the Giants*, *The Letters*, *The Psalms and Prayers*. In his establishment of scripture and his missionary journeys, he is more reminiscent of Muhammad than Jesus. Like Muhammad, he acknowledged the validity of earlier religions but considered himself and his teachings to be the heir and fulfilment of them, and himself to be the last prophet.

In 274, Bahram I took over as king of Babylon, and this coincided with the Magi, the powerful priestly caste of the Zoroastrian religion, becoming more influential. The head of the Magi, one Kartir or Kerder, became a deadly opponent of Mani and his teaching. Bahram, the king, put Mani into prison and had him executed after 26 days. He justified Mani's imprisonment and execution by claiming that it was necessary to destroy him before Mani destroyed the entire world. Perhaps this fear was prompted by some apocalyptic claim of Mani's. His corpse was flayed and the stuffed body was placed on show outside the city as a warning. Many of Mani's pupils, and their pupils too, were martyred.

Although Manichaeanism suffered persecution in its homeland, it had quickly spread to Syria and Palestine, Egypt, North Africa and Rome. It was in North Africa and Italy that Augustine of Hippo practised Manichaeanism. Augustine was ironically both the most famous convert to Manichaeanism and its most famous apostate. Augustine's polemics against Manichaeanism are voluminous and Augustine's own theology was influenced by the Manichaean doctrine of his youth.

Christianity saw Manichaeanism as a dangerous competitor, but once again, Christianity was the victor in the contest. From the sixth century on, the influence of Manichaeanism waned, and it quickly died out in the West. But it remained successful in central Asia, particularly in Turkestan. In 762 CE it actually became the state religion of the Uigar empire in Mongolia, maintaining its position until the empire's collapse in 840 CE, upon which, the Manichaean religion went through a period of persecution in China.

In central Asia it continued alongside Buddhism and Nestorian Christianity until the Mongol invasions wiped it out. Or so it was believed until recent research suggested that the last evidence for Manichaeans seemed to be in seventeenth-century China, according to a Portuguese report. As Hans Jonas put it, 'Mani's is the only Gnostic system which became a broad historical force... Mani intended to found a universal religion, not merely a sect available only to the few.'[50]

Mani was careful to put his teachings into writing, so Manichaean teachings have survived. For some reason, Gnosticism finds its expression in literature rather than in the visual arts or in buildings. Because the religion flourished and declined successively in different areas, and because the 'religion of light' died out and was not valued by any successive religions or teachings, surviving Manichaeism texts are in a wide variety of languages, from Greek and Coptic to Iranian, Old Turkish and Chinese.

As always, our main sources of information on the Manichaeans themselves (rather than their scriptures) are from heresy-hunting opponents such as Augustine of Hippo, and the later Theodore ben Konai. Arabic writers also refer to them. However, major caches of Manichaean texts were found at Turfan in China and Fayum in Egypt. We also have many fragments of texts, but few complete books. In comparison with the Nag

Hammadi literature, Manichaean studies have been relatively neglected, the timing of the manuscript discoveries by Westerners being less fortuitous than the Nag Hammadi Library or the Dead Sea Scrolls. The Manichaean material is also that much further away from Western interest, but over the last couple of decades Manichaean experts have taken leaps forward in the publication and translation of texts and in the interpretation and reconstruction of Manichaean lifestyle and doctrine.

Mani's dualism is an absolute dualism, probably inherited from Zoroastrianism. It has a starker contrast than the mitigated dualism of the Sethians or Valentinians. In Manichaean cosmology there are two eternal principles, one light and one dark, which represent quite a different scheme, with quite different possibilities, from the Gnostic system of true God and demiurge. For Manichaeans, darkness or evil was there from the beginning, whereas for Sethian or Valentinian Gnostics it was a result of a fall from the Pleroma, usually as a result of Sophia's unnatural curiosity or wrongful coupling with lower elements.

With the exception of the Mongolian Uigar empire, Manichaeans were in a minority and were an unofficial religion wherever they went. Also, Manichaeans regarded Jesus, Buddha and Zoroaster as all being prophets and saviours, even though their teachings were regarded as incomplete in comparison to Mani's. Thus the Manichaeans had a tendency to adapt their teachings to the local official religions, such as Christianity or Buddhism or Zoroastrianism. Mani is given titles that mark him as the fulfilment of all three religions: he is the Paraclete of the Gospel of John (John 14:16, 26), the messianic son of Zoroaster and the Maitreya Buddha. As the Manichaean text, the Kephalaia, puts it:

'The writings and the wisdom and the apoca-
lypses and the parables and the psalms of all
earlier churches were gathered everywhere and
came to my church and were added to the wisdom
which I revealed.'[51]

Moses and the Old Testament prophets are notably absent from
the list of Mani's predecessors, but Seth, sometimes called Seth
ēl, the third son of Adam and Eve who was so important to the
Sethian Gnostics, was acknowledged as an important revealer
figure, one of the 'apostles of light', as were Noah, Enosh, Enoch,
and even Abraham. Paul was also a respected figure, as he was
for many Gnostics, and the entire list of revealer figures and
apostles is very Gnostic.

Manichaeanism was strong in Syria, and the Manichaeans
inherited some of the heterodox traditions of Syrian Christianity.
Quotations and images that are clearly from the *Gospel of Thomas*
appear in Manichaean literature. For instance Thomas 19 refers
to the 'five trees in Paradise, which do not move in summer nor
in winter, and their leaves do not fall down. Whoever knows them
will not taste death.' These five trees, interpreted as reason,
thinking, insight, speculation and reflection, which are all
elements of gnosis, have an important role in Manichaean myth.
Mani may even have modelled his missionary journeys on those
ascribed to the apostle Thomas in the apocryphal *Acts of Thomas*.

A collection of Manichaean hymns entitled *The Psalms of
Thomas* refers to a pupil of Mani named Thomas, not to the
apostle, but quotations from the *Gospel of Thomas* are embedded
in various Manichaean texts. The *Hymn of the Pearl*, included in
two manuscripts of the *Acts of Thomas*, is Gnostic but of

unknown origin, and some scholars (such as Johan Ferreira) have argued that it is Manichaean in origin. The Gnostic techniques of myth, allegory and reinterpretation are central to Manichaean teaching.

The surviving Manichaean sources are mostly post sixth century, and this makes it difficult to work out how much of the teaching belongs to Mani himself rather than his successors. But this is a common problem in religious history – we have good historical information on later phases of the religions but only legendary or sparse information on the founders themselves. In addition to the common saviour/redeemer figures, many of the mythical characters and entities of classical Gnosticism carry through to Mani's versions. Cosmogonies – myths of creation – are important. There are aeons and archons, respectively emanations from the God of light and from darkness. There are two principles in the world, light and darkness, or good and evil. The god of light created other beings, aeons (*shekinah* in the Syriac, like the word that is used for the feminine presence of God in the Kabbalah), which exist in an orderly universe.

Manichaeanism was commonly known as 'the religion of light' or 'the teaching of light' and the Manichaean concept of light was an overwhelming concern for them. Manichaean practices, such as consuming certain vegetables in the belief that this would allow the fallen light particles within them to be liberated, can only really be understood if the underlying mythology is understood.

Their creation myth has three stages, the initial, eternal co-existence of light and dark, followed by the attack of darkness on the light and the subsequent mixing of light and dark, and then thirdly the continuing efforts of the light to extract light from darkness.

In the beginning, there was light and darkness, coexisting in an absolute dualism. Manichaeanism tended towards a very concrete symbolism, and in a manner somewhat reminiscent of Blake's prophetic poems, metaphysical aspects are assigned to the points of the compass. The realm of light is located in the north, the realm of darkness in the south. These locations seem counter-intuitive, and east and west would seem to be more suitable, since the sun rises in the east and sets in the west, unless perhaps the placement of light in the north somehow refers to the 'white nights' of high summer in the far north. God, or the Father of Greatness, or King of the Paradise of Light, has a realm that is orderly and consists of the five chief aeons, but is surrounded by innumerable other aeons and worlds.

Darkness, the realm of Hyle or matter, also has its king, a composite creature whose lion head indicates that he is a development of the Gnostic demiurge Ialdabaoth. The Manichaean mythology and system are full of fives, or pentads, and the realm of darkness, which on one level is our own world, is composed of five worlds – smoke, fire, the breeze (or sirocco), water, darkness. Each of these worlds is ruled by an archon. The opposed aeons and archons are obviously straight from the earlier Gnostics, but the absolute dualism of Mani creates an interesting distinction to the other systems and thus these entities fit into the grand scheme rather differently.

In the earlier Gnostic systems the aeons are inarguably higher than the archons, being part of the Pleroma and existing before the fall of Sophia, who is herself an aeon. For the earlier Gnostics, the archons are a result of the demiurge's rule of our world, and escape from this world into the Pleroma is an escape from the tyranny of the archons. In the Manichaean system, the aeons and archons are equally ancient and are pitched against each other: five major aeons of light versus five major archons of darkness. This absolute dualism leads to a quite different mythical and psychological emphasis. Although the principles of light and darkness have eternally coexisted, our world, in which the two are combined, was a subsequent creation. It contains both light and darkness and, through a somewhat complex process, was the result of the meeting or clash of light and darkness.

Darkness was in the south and light in the north, but in the middle these two principles or kingdoms bordered on each other, and darkness began to fight against light. The King of Light was not able to fight the darkness directly because 'God had nothing evil with which to chastise Matter, for in the house of God there is nothing evil.'[52] The darkness was by its nature chaotic, lawless, hateful. 'Strife and bitterness belong to the nature of its parts.'[53] So the King of Light created three 'evocations' – Wisdom or the Great Spirit, from whom was issued the Mother of All Living (utilizing a further version of the Gnostic trinity). She then brought forward Man, the primal, archetypal man whose Living Soul also consisted of five elements, fire, wind, water, light and ether.[54]

The Man proceeds to fight the darkness and is defeated, but this is merely a ploy to infiltrate Hyle, the world of matter. 'Thereupon the Primal Man gave himself and his five sons as food to the five sons of darkness, as a man who has an enemy mixes a deadly poison in a cake and gives it to him.'[55]

The Living Soul of Man is then 'blind and deaf, unconscious and confused', unaware of its true origin. But the darkness has been to some extent satiated by this absorption of light and ceases its attack on the realm of light.

In the next stage, the King of Light sends out another Man, who is the Living Spirit rather than the Living Soul and is not intended to be taken down into the darkness. The Living Spirit communicates with the Living Soul, who is trapped in matter. The Spirit sends a call of awakening to the Soul, to which the Soul replies, and the Spirit eventually enables the Soul to free itself from matter. Put so baldly, we can see the same relationship between soul and spirit that was so evident in the earlier Gnostic systems, particularly Valentinianism – a relationship that we discussed in Chapter 2. The spirit is eternally connected to the light and doing the work of the King of Light. But (even though in the Manichaean system it comes from the realm of the light rather than the demiurge) the soul is absorbed by the dark and is susceptible to the influence of matter.

The gist of this is identical to the story of the soul in texts like the *Exegesis on the Soul*, in which the female soul falls from her home in the house of the father down to the body and matter, is ravished and seduced by thieves and adulterers, but is filled with remorse and then hears the call of the father and is united with the bridegroom. Once again, the elaborate Gnostic cosmology and cosmogony also constitutes a system of psychology or anthropology and in the Manichaean mythology has a personal meaning in addition to a cosmic one.

The soul is a bait to matter. It is trapped in matter but it then acts as an intermediary between matter and spirit because it can turn again towards the spirit. In some Manichaean texts, the soul is a lamb or a maiden, a false sacrifice that subverts the darkness which claims it. The means by which the Living Spirit aids the Living Soul is a model for the liberation and salvation of all humankind from Adam onwards.

But this entire foregoing creation story occurred before the formation of our own world. The Living Soul descended into darkness itself, not into an intermediate world, and the five elements of the Living Soul are still trapped in matter. So the Living Spirit sets into motion the creation of our world (this is in effect crafted by a demiurge, but not an ignorant, illegitimate demiurge – Saklas and Nebroel, names of the demiurge in other traditions, occur as demons in the Manichaean myth). The world is therefore a combination of light and darkness, but was created in an attempt to liberate the particles of light (trapped in the form of the five elements) from the world.

So there is light in almost everything in this world. It is the light within the human soul that is the most important to liberate, but a secondary transformation involves liberating the light in other creatures, from plant to animal. Some plants, fruit and vegetables were seen as containing more light than most, and the Perfect ate these so that they could liberate the light particles from them. This is probably tied in with the feeling that a diet of vegetables like cucumbers, fruit like melons or grapes creates a light energy in humans, and one can sense an element of the assessment of the yin and yang qualities of food that is important in diets such as the macrobiotic, succulent fruits being light within the Manichaean tradition, and meat being dark.

The five sons of the Living Spirit maintain the cosmos, which consists of ten firmaments and eight earthly spheres and exists expressly for the purpose of liberating the light.

A third and final 'evocation' is created and the King of Light's plan for rescuing the particles of light is complete, though it is ongoing. The third evocation is known as the third envoy, or third messenger, but also, confusingly, as God of the Realm of

Light and the Great Architect, though he is not identical with the original King of Light. The third envoy has astrological characteristics; he lives in the sun and has as his virgin daughters the 12 houses of the zodiac. Three wheels of fire, water and wind refine and purify the particles of light that form a column or pillar of glory, visible to mankind as the Milky Way. Light from the column of glory fills up the moon, which waxes as light is added to it and wanes as the light is discharged.[56] When the particles of soul-light are discharged they make their way to the New Aeon, designed by the Great Architect (the third envoy) as a new kingdom or home for the rescued light.

The next stage of the myth is expressed in bizarre sexual imagery. It should be remembered that the Manichaean Perfects or Elect were celibate and that sex was perceived by them as an activity that imprisoned light. The third envoy revealed himself as both male and female in order to attract the archons of the darkness, who had light trapped in them. These archons could not copulate with the third envoy, but were sexually excited even so and either masturbated or brought forth abortions. These sexual products fell to earth, the semen producing plants when it fell on dry earth but giving rise to a sea monster when it fell into the sea. The aborted embryos fell onto dry land as demons, ate the fruit of the plants produced by the semen and became animals. Thus there are three classes of creature – plants, animals and demons – that contain light particles, all of which precede humans and are the result of the inability of the archons to copulate with the androgynous third envoy.

In the penultimate stage, the realm of darkness makes a counter move. Two demons, Saklas and Nebroel (interestingly the *Gospel of Judas* uses both of these names for the demiurge, so the Manichaeans must have drawn on Sethian Gnostic traditions), create Adam and Eve. The demons and the light within these two demons are absorbed into Adam and Eve so that the future of the world depends on humanity. The third envoy reacts to this move by sending the 'Jesus Splendour', a revealer figure, to Adam. The Jesus Splendour gives Adam the knowledge of all that has gone before the creation of Adam and Eve, and of their situation in the universe. Thus the Jesus Splendour represents gnosis.

The Jesus Splendour in turn summons the Mind of Light or Light-nous, the father of the apostles or divine messengers. The five gifts of the Light-nous help the soul to become conscious of itself and help it to resist the darkness, yet another example of the importance of soul and spirit in Gnosticism. Thus the world and the entire physical universe is a device for liberating or harvesting light particles, a machine for transforming energies. The body belongs to the darkness, and as long as the soul has not awakened, it is continually reincarnated in successive bodies. Once it awakens it can make its way to the realm of light via the column of glory. This version of reincarnation, or metempsychosis, quite probably came from Buddhism, but reincarnation itself was not unknown to other Gnostics or early Christians. It resurfaces in the Cathars, who may have got it directly or indirectly from the Manichaeans.

The harvesting of light will continue until nearly all of the light is liberated, and then Jesus will come as king, the world will be dissolved and the remaining particles of trapped light will be freed. Light will once again be separated from darkness, but the darkness will no longer be able to encroach on the light.

Many aspects of the Manichaean myth might seem bizarre to

our Western sensibilities but there is a beauty to the grand scheme. Imagine being able to look up at the night sky and see the column of glory visible as the Milky Way, a divine symbol of the liberation of light from darkness, and to look at the waxing moon as particles of the liberated light fill it up, to see the sun as the home of the third evocation.

Manichaeism was a religion, and like Christianity it had prayers, psalms and hymns. Many of the hymns address the mythical characters described in the stories, such as the Mother of All Living, or the Great Architect, or even the Column of Light. These are devout prayers, psalms and hymns that recount the myths and appeal to the entities in much the same way that Christians might appeal to Jesus or Mary. The myths were not only psychological schemes for the Manichaeans but were imbued with a sense of emotion and religious reality.

In Manichaeanism, the creation of the world is thus not wrong or the result of a mistake, but an inevitable result of the eternal existence of light and darkness. A spark of light, of God, is hidden within man and thus man has a responsibility for returning all of the imprisoned light to God. The world itself contains light, which can be successfully separated from the darkness. The entire process can be viewed in the night sky, apparent only to Manichaeans. Perhaps this is one of the factors that enabled Manichaeanism to become a long-lasting religion rather than a more temporary teaching.

Manichaeanism was a widespread religion that lasted for over a millennium, so it became somewhat more formalized than most Gnostic movements. That kind of formalization is in turn a movement away from gnosis itself towards praxis – towards certain standards of behaviour, towards rituals which must be

practised in order to achieve salvation, towards dogma and stan-
dardization. Yet the concept of gnosis still continued to have a
central role in Manichaeanism, whether or not the experiencing
of it truly continued (and it is always difficult to judge whether
a historical movement was truly experiencing and living the
spiritual truths that it proclaimed). In principle, gnosis was what
could save mankind while praxis could save the other beings,
plants and animals in the world.

* * *

Manichaeans were divided into a hierarchy of Hearers (auditors)
who could live ordinary lives, and the Perfect or the Elect, who
were under severe restrictions. This division was bequeathed
to the later Bogomils and Cathars. The Perfect or Elect themselves
were organized into a hierarchy, at the pinnacle of which was
the 'head' of the Church, seen as a successor to Mani, the
12 apostles, 72 deacons or bishops, 360 elders and then the
ordinary Elect. Women could become Elect or Perfect, but could
not hold office.

The Elect were ordained in ceremonies that involved a laying
on of hands, which was possibly passed on to the Cathars as the
rite of the consolamentum. They were strict vegetarians, were
forbidden to lie, were celibate and were restricted in the kinds
of work that they could do. Every living being was considered
to contain some of the light, and ill-treating or damaging a living
being, or even polluting the water, was seen as an act that could
torment the light within. Thus the Perfect were careful not to kill
insects, and walked with their eyes facing the ground lest they
accidentally trod on a weed or a blade of grass. Their extreme
care in avoiding causing suffering to other living beings is
reminiscent of Jainism or some forms of Buddhism.

The Perfect fasted for 100 days a year, the longest fast lasting for a challenging 30 days that led up to the commemoration of Mani's death, the Manichaean equivalent of Easter. They lived a monk-like existence and had to dedicate a large amount of their time to the copying and translating of Manichaean texts; they were known as skilled and careful scribes. There were Manichaean monasteries, probably modelled after Buddhist forms rather than Christian.

The Hearers could perform the necessary actions of life that the Elect were banned from doing, such as working and preparing food, so the Elect were dependent on the Hearers for their everyday needs. Paradoxically these very actions that the Hearers performed for the Elect prevented them from achieving redemption in this lifetime.

The Manichaeans believed in reincarnation and, like the Cathars, believed that the outer circle of Manichaeans could only achieve redemption in the next lifetime. The light particles present in a Hearer would be transmitted in the next lifetime to a Perfect or, curiously, could be incarnated to one of the plants considered to be full of light. It seems strange that a Hearer might base his hope for salvation on the chance of becoming a melon or cucumber in his next life.

When Manichaeans met each other, they clasped their right hands. This practice referred to a myth, where the right hand was extended by the Mother of All Living to the Primal Man (or Living Soul) when he went to his defeat in the first war, but it was also extended to the Primal Man by the Living Spirit when he helped him out of the war, or the darkness.

The body belonged to the darkness, but the Manichaeans did not only practise a simple rejection of the body; they were careful to treat the body correctly, according to their beliefs. Hearers were also restricted by ten commandments. According to Rudolph these were 'monogamy, the renunciation of fornication, lying, hypocrisy, idolatry, magic, the killing of animals, theft and any doubt of their religion, as well as the duty of the indefatigable care of the Elect.'[57]

Although the Elect were careful not to accidentally injure plants, and were not allowed to eat meat, great importance was placed on consuming vegetables that were considered to contain a large amount of light. Daily communal meals consisted of bread and water or fruit juice, plus succulent vegetables such as cucumbers or figs or melons. All of these were considered to contain light, and the Perfect were extracting and transforming the light particles by consuming this food – cleansing the light of the dark matter that surrounded it, refining and digesting it so that the light could be returned to its rightful home.

* * *

The Manichaean religion, the religion of light, was unusual in many ways. It was universalist and spread through three continents, a feat equalled only by the major world religions. It was long lived for a Gnostic movement, its lifetime matched or exceeded only by the Mandaeans, who were always an exclusive group who did not attract converts. Manichaeanism absorbed other Gnostic teachings along with the teachings of Christ, Zoroaster and Buddha, and it bequeathed aspects of its mythology, dualism and organization to the Bogomils and the Cathars, the two major Christian 'heresies' that were to enliven and enlighten Eastern and Western Europe respectively in the Middle Ages.

Its roots stretched down to the third-century figure of Mani, a genuine historical figure, the founder of a major religion, who, like Muhammad, claimed to be dispensing the final revelations, of which previous teachings and religions had given only partial accounts. And now they are gone. There are no more Manichaeans, just as there are no more Valentinians or Sethians or Cathars or Bogomils. Surely the teachings of Mani and the religion of light are among the great ignored spiritual traditions of the West, or indeed of the world, and deserve the renewed attention of genuine spiritual seekers such as the Gnostics and Cathars have received.

But Mani is still remembered in tradition, if vaguely. In a remote part of southern China, a single Manichaean temple had survived at least into the late nineteenth century. Once China had opened up to outside influences again in the 1990s, a team of UNESCO-backed researchers were able to visit the temple and to confirm that the statue now worshipped as Buddha was in fact a Chinese statue of Mani. The Chinese name for Buddha is actually Muni, which is written identically in the Chinese script, and so it was easy for the identity of one God (as Mani was considered to be) to be replaced by another. The researchers discovered that there were further statues of Mani in private houses in the area. So despite the persecutions and the ravages of time, Mani is still remembered in a far corner of China.[58]

CHAPTER 8

THE VARIETY AND
TRANSMISSION
OF GNOSIS

The Manichaean religion had become a storehouse of Gnosticism, and its diffusion into so many parts of the Asian-European world allowed it to transmit Gnostic influence in the difficult centuries after the Roman Empire had accepted Christianity. Its status as a separate religion from Christianity enabled Gnostic ideas and texts to be preserved despite Christianity's developing intolerance for 'heresy'. Manichaeanism bridged the gap between the ancient Gnostic sects and the 'heretical' dualist forms of medieval Christianity like the Paulicians, Bogomils and Cathars.

Manichaeans revered Zoroaster and Buddha in addition to Mani and Jewish and Christian figures, so their attitude to the world could spread by osmosis when they encountered Buddhists and Zoroastrians. While we tend to think of religions as giant monolithic entities, in reality all religion is local religion. French Catholicism has different tendencies to Italian

Catholicism, and Catholicism in Rome is different to Catholicism in Milan, Catholicism in the Republic of Ireland is different to Catholicism in Northern Ireland. There are always splinter groups and strange amalgams of different faiths, such as the Taoist Christians in China who produced the Jesus sutras. Unique sects like the Mandaeans, Yezidis or Druze were able to survive in the diversity of culture and religion that comprised central Asia and the Levant.

While Western European Christendom entered the so-called Dark Ages, other areas and religions were developing their own forms of Gnosticism. Whether these new forms were historically influenced by the Gnostics is not clear in every case. We find resemblances to ancient Gnostic ideas in Jewish Gnosis, Mahayana Buddhism, Advaita Vedanta, Neoplatonism and Islamic Gnosis. Some of these religious movements, such as Kabbalah and Neoplatonism, clearly encountered the Gnostics or the Manichaeans, others probably developed similar views independently.

Mystical experience does not necessarily result in a Gnostic world view. The Catholic mystics like St John of the Cross or Teresa of Avila found the dogma and theology of Catholic Christianity to be an adequate framework to explain and nurture their spiritual experiences. We should be careful not to label every mystical, spiritual or esoteric teaching as Gnostic. There are surely many points of similarity in alchemical teachings, Rosicrucianism, the esoteric side of freemasonry, or in aspects of the Western occult tradition, but, to my mind at least, these are not truly Gnostic in their outlook.[59]

Christianity did not lose all of its mystical aspirations when the Gnostic sects were exiled and suppressed. The writings of the

Eastern fathers collected by the Orthodox Church as the Philokalia are a mine of esoteric Christianity. They practised allegorical interpretation, were ascetic, used Hesychastic practices like unceasing prayer and breathing techniques, and their principle of theogony, man becoming God, would have appealed to many Gnostics. Some of the early Fathers in the Philokalia were heterodox and at times were considered heretical. But gnosis itself was not central to their form of Christianity, and it was faith that defined the Christian mystic. Dogma was important and the writers of the Philokalia were careful not to overstep the boundaries of acceptable Christian thought and belief. No writer in the Philokalia could invert the values of the Bible or suggest that the story of the Garden of Eden was simply an episode in a greater cosmic drama.

* * *

Even the barest outline of Jewish Kabbalah (let alone occultist Christian Kabbalah) or of its history is beyond the scope of this book, so the following few paragraphs take the briefest of glances at the historical and systematic connections between Kabbalah and Gnosticism.

The Zohar was claimed to have been written in the second century CE, at the same period as the Gnostic literature. Recent scholarship, however, has suggested that primary works such as the Zohar were written in the late medieval period. Even so, Kabbalah had a precursor contemporary to the ancient Gnostics in Merkabah or 'throne' mysticism.

Merkabah mysticism developed the ascent of the soul, basing the visionary experience on a meditation of the chariot described in the book of Ezekiel. In later Kabbalah, this visionary ascent became adapted to the sephiroth of the tree of life, an emanationist theology that has obvious similarities to the Gnostic systems. Affinities have been noted between the baptismal Elkasaites and the adherents of Merkabah mysticism. The Elkasaites possibly had Gnostic connections, and Mani was born into an Elkasaite community in the third century.[60]

In some early rabbinical reports, there are hints of 'two powers in heaven' that suggest the role of a demiurge, and in his writings Philo of Alexandria sometimes adapts the Platonic concept of a demiurgic creator. Although these Jewish ideas were later viewed as heretical, they do suggest parallel developments between the ancient Gnostics and esoteric Jewish groups who remained under the umbrella of Judaism.

The mythical transmission of the Kabbalah goes through the line from Adam to Seth to Noah to Shem, then from Melchizedek to Abraham and on, or from Enoch... many of these names are familiar to us as mythical conductors of the Gnostic tradition. The earliest forms of Kabbalah thus share historical and philosophical roots with the ancient Gnostics.

* * *

Neoplatonism is the last stage of the Platonic tradition, though the term may cover the philosophy in a historical period from the third century to the Renaissance. Plotinus (c.205–70 CE) was the first Neoplatonist, and his philosophy treated the spiritual universe as having separate levels of soul, mind or Nous and the One. The One was the godhead, the highest principle who, as with the Gnostics, could only be described as what he was not. Neoplatonism had many overlaps with Gnostic thought, not least in that it stressed the importance of personal spiritual experience.

'The novice must hold himself constantly under
some image of the Divine Being and seek in the

> light of a clear conception; knowing thus, in a
> deep conviction, whither he is going – into what a
> sublimity he penetrates – he must give himself
> forthwith to the inner and, radiant with the
> Divine Intellections (with which he is now one),
> be no longer the seer, but, as that place has made
> him, the seen.'[61]

The Sethian Gnostics may, as John Turner has suggested, have aligned themselves more with Neoplatonic thought once the hostility of Christianity had become overwhelming. In many ways, the Neoplatonists were more part of the establishment than the Gnostics. The Gnostics were related to a Church that rejected them, whereas the Neoplatonists were able to be the transmitters of Platonic philosophy, in a tradition that stretched back for centuries. Neoplatonists and Gnostics were not in accord over many points; Plotinus included a diatribe against the Gnostics in his *Enneads*. He criticized the Gnostics for their jargon, for their unacknowledged debt to Plato, for the idea that the world was created after a fall and that the fallen state of the world is equivalent to the fallen state of the human soul. The unsystematic mythical presentation of the Gnostics is particularly troublesome to the philosopher Plotinus, who placed great weight on the rational, intellectual exposition of spiritual experience.

As Christianity took over the Roman Empire, Neoplatonism came to be seen as a last hope for the classical pagan religion. Plotinus' brand of Neoplatonism was too intellectual to have a wide appeal, and it was the later Neoplatonist Iamblichus (250–325 CE) who to some extent popularized Neoplatonism.

Julian the Apostate, the emperor who briefly reversed the flow and reinstated paganism as the official religion of the Roman Empire, believed that the philosophy of Iamblichus exceeded that of Plato. Iamblichus' system brought austere Neoplatonism into contact with the ritual and magical elements of paganism. He produced a teaching that acknowledged the ultimate aim of gnosis of the One but allowed the practitioner to partake of pagan ritual and magical practice. As such it became the dominant form of Neoplatonism.

Neoplatonism was banned within Christendom in 529 CE, and the Neoplatonist schools in Alexandria and Athens were closed, but its influence lingered well into the medieval period and it was revived along with the Hermetic philosophy in the Renaissance.

* * *

It is not only in the West or the near East that we find religious and spiritual movements that have a strong familial resemblance to Gnosticism. Advaita Vedanta is the non-dualistic interpretation of the Hindu Vedas. Non-dualism means that there is no difference between the soul of the individual human being and the soul of Brahma, the highest divine being. In ancient Gnosticism, the spirit is akin to the Pleroma and to God, and knowledge of God is obtained through knowledge of oneself, so self-knowledge is knowledge of God. The material world is *maya*, an illusion that is the result of transcendental ignorance. Sanskrit is an Indo-European language, as are Greek and English, and the word *jnana* is cognate with gnosis. In the Rig Veda creation is described in Emanationist terms, and the One does not give rise to creation directly, just as in the Gnostic systems. There is also a primal man similar to the anthropos, and the influence of the many Gods of Hindu religion is often regarded as malign in a similar way to the Gnostic idea of Fate or Heimarmene.[62]

Although the Vedas are thought to have been written before the Common Era, Advaita itself is dated to the eighth century CE. Therefore any direct historical connection between Advaita and ancient Gnosticism must run from Gnosticism to Advaita. Conversely, Gnosticism may have been influenced by the Upanishads themselves, or this may be a case of parallel development.

Similarly, in Mahayana Buddhism we find many features in common with Gnosticism. Salvation depends on gnosis, not on faith or deeds, and the world is characterized by being in a state of ignorance. The importance of divine feminine figures like Barbelo or Sophia is mirrored in Buddhism. The scholar Edward Conze has proposed a list of parallels between Gnosticism and Mahayana Buddhism which include: elitism, use of myth, wisdom as a god and as a human attribute, antinomianism, the contrast between the ultimate God and a demiurge (Mara in Buddhism), an esoteric outlook and, despite the dualism so prevalent in the material world, an essential monistic outlook.

* * *

The Sufis, the spiritual side of Islam, have fascinated Westerners for a long time. Even before the evangelizing efforts of Idries Shah in the 1960s and the elevation of Hafiz and Rumi to the status of the most popular poets in the USA, Persian and Arabic poets exerted a fascination on the West. The Sufis were themselves called Gnostics, 'knowers', at various times, and the poetic imagery of the lover and beloved that occurs so frequently in the poetry is clearly reminiscent of the bridal chamber imagery that is so prominent in Valentinianism.

Islam considered itself to be the successor to Judaism and Christianity, and they believed that Muhammad was, like Mani, the last of a series of prophets. Muhammad's declaration of himself as the final prophet might even have been derived directly or indirectly from Mani's similar view of himself, but Muhammad's spiritual forebears were all Jewish and Christian, and, unlike Manichaeism, there was no space for Buddha or Zoroaster in Islam.

Muhammad certainly knew Jews and Christians and their traditions. Some of the Qur'an's versions of stories related to Jesus are derived from apocryphal and Gnostic Christian texts. The stories in the Qur'an in which Mary gives birth to Jesus beneath a palm tree, and in which Jesus makes birds out of clay are also found in the apocryphal infancy gospels. The Qur'anic view that Jesus was not actually crucified is well known in Gnostic texts, for example in *The Second Treatise of the Great Seth*, and has its roots in Docetism. It has also been suggested that Muhammad had contact with Merkabah mysticism. Additionally, Muhammad ascended through seven spheres, which is immediately reminiscent of the Gnostic ascent of the soul.

Gnostic influence on Islam is not represented only in the Qur'an. The Islamicist Carl Ernst has recently shown that *The Hymn of the Pearl*, the beautiful tale of fall and redemption that has survived in the West only in the *Acts of Thomas*, was well known in Islamic cultures. Ernst has found versions of it in Arabic, Persian, Turkish and Urdu.[63] There are also echoes of the hymn's themes and story in other Sufi literature. Each of these translations is based on a version found in a Hindu text on hatha yoga known as the *Amrtakunda* or *The Pool of Nectar*, testifying also to Gnostic influence in India. The surviving texts are found in many locations, mainly in Turkey, and usually in the possession of Sufi orders, including the Mevlevi dervishes.

While there may be many points of similarity between mystical Sufi poetry and philosophy, the religious framework of the Sufis is Islamic, and many features of Gnostic doctrine do not sit any easier within mainstream Islam than they do in mainstream Christianity. To Muslims, Allah is the only God and the notion of a separate demiurge who is worshipped as a God, even if he is considered a false or ignorant God, is a blasphemous one. But there are earlier strains of Islam that do contain such notions. It has even been suggested that 'Gnostic adaptations to Islam were so extensive in the eighth century that "these assertive reorganizing movements constitute a virtual failed takeover of Islam".'[64]

Islamic Gnosticism has been identified mainly with Ghulat and Ismaili Muslims. After Muhammad's death, Islam experienced schism. When Muhammad's cousin Ali and his sons were murdered, the Sh'ite branch of Islam followed the descendants of Ali. The Ghulat were early Shi'ites, and so were the Ismailis. The Ghulat, or 'extremists', are so called because of the extreme importance, which according to their opponents almost amounted to idolatry, that they gave to the members of Muhammad's family.

The Ismaili get their name from their acceptance of Ismail bin Jafar as the divinely appointed spiritual successor (Imam) to Jafar al-Sadiq, wherein they differ from the Twelvers, who accept Musa al-Kazim, younger brother of Ismail, as the true Imam. The Ismaili and the Twelvers both accept the same initial Imams from the descendants of Muhammad through his daughter Fatima Zahra and therefore share much of their early history, but the

Ismailis accept only seven imams as successors of Muhammad.

In an early Ismaili creation myth, God created light, which was not only the quality of light, but also a living creature. This existed in eternity for a long time, not knowing whether it was the creator itself (rather like Philip Pullman's Authority, who was the first-emerged being in the universe, but, despite his claims, did not create the universe). Eventually, God created breath into it and commanded 'Be', which gave the feminine name Kuni to the creature. God commanded Kuni to create Qadar as a helper for herself. In some early sources, Kuni and Qadar were interpreted as intellect and soul, a very common Gnostic relation of myth to personal spiritual makeup. From these two, Kuni and Qadar, were emanated another seven beings, called cherubim, and then a further twelve spiritual beings that were seen as mediating between Kuni and the prophet (Muhammad) and the imams.

This emanationist theology, seemingly very un-Muslim, is obviously quite Gnostic in its formation. The female Kuni 'gave off a proud thought', which had unfortunate repercussions later, reminiscent of the arrogance of the demiurge or the fall of Sophia. Like the ancient Gnostics, Ismaili gnosis denigrates the material world, which was created last of all, although the material world was modelled after the spiritual in the 'as above, so below' principle.

The Mother of Books is a Ghulat text with Gnostic affinities. It contains such Gnostic tropes as the five trees in Paradise, which are known in Thomas 19 and in Manichaean literature. Azaz'il, the world creator, is incompetent and rebels and thus suffers a fall. The five special lights in *The Mother of Books* resemble the five angels in Sethian literature. Secret knowledge of the creation of the world is important in this text. *The Mother of Books* is explicitly Gnostic in the following: 'The one who knows arises and testifies to spirit as to himself.'[65]

The Ghulats and Ismailis are chief amongst the Islamic sects usually considered as Gnostic, but there are others. The Alawites are Shi'ite Muslims in Syria who may have predated Islam and whose beliefs may have Gnostic elements. The Druze are also Muslim related, but are often not considered to be true Muslims by the more orthodox. They are also located in Syria, as well as in Lebanon, Jordan and Israel. The Druze are divided into two castes: a secular caste, who are called 'the ignorant', and a religious caste called 'the knowers' or Gnostics. Their cosmology is Emanationist and they believe in reincarnation. Their use of the Qur'an involves some esoteric interpretation.

* * *

As the first millennium CE drew to a close, Western Manichaeism had declined but there were still many heterodox Christian groups in the near East. Armenia was host to many unusual groups over the centuries, including archontic and Valentinian Gnostics, and strange sects such as the Yezidis still had a presence there well into the twentieth century.

The Paulicians may represent a historical link in the chain of dualism between the Manichaeans and the Bogomils. Our material on the Paulicians is very sparse, so there is little direct evidence that gnosis itself was important to them. Was the experience of gnosis there, dwelling silently at the centre, left out of the heresy-hunting accounts which focused on doctrines that could easily be labelled as heretical? Perhaps we shall never know. Their beliefs have some clear links with Marcionism and with Bogomilism and Catharism after them.

The late scholar Ioan Couliano and others have argued that the link between the Paulicians and the Bogomils is not a historical one, of an older sect directly influencing a new sect, but may simply be explained by the *ideas* or *system* of dualism coming back to life spontaneously. There are only so many ways of looking at the world, and of reading the Bible, and the dualist interpretation, with or without the concept or gnosis, is one of them. So it follows that different peoples in different times, but perhaps in somewhat similar circumstances, will come independently to a dualistic version of Christianity. Also, there were dualistic elements in surviving apocryphal literature and in Plato. That said there were enough dualist or Gnostic influences in the area for us to imagine a direct transmission, even if there is no hard evidence.

In surviving accounts, the Paulicians are condemned as people who believe in two principles, good and evil, light and night, and believe that the devil is the creator of this world.[66]

If the principle of the demiurge is adapted back into mainstream Christianity, the figure of the devil or Lucifer or Satan is obviously the prime candidate for the job. The Paulicians were also Docetists, and they believed that Mary had no part in the character of Jesus, that he descended into her and was brought out in childbirth, going through her 'as if through a pipe' without his spiritual quality touching her in any way. This belief is held in common with some Bogomils and Cathars. Neither did the Paulicians believe that Mary was a virgin, quite reasonably citing the siblings of Jesus mentioned in the gospels – James, Joses, Jude, Simon and unnamed sisters – as evidence that Mary's hymen was unlikely to be intact. It was claimed that the Paulicians themselves rejected marriage.

The Paulicians also rejected the Mosaic Law and the Old Testament and they did not believe in the transubstantiation of the host during the Eucharist but read the bread and wine allegorically as referring to the two sets of scripture important to them: the Gospels and the Letters of the Apostle Paul. Baptism was interpreted symbolically and not practised. Their New Testament was the same as the Catholic canon, except that they rejected the Petrine epistles, seeing Peter as a false apostle who was responsible for the success of the false Catholic Orthodox. Later they seem to have stripped the canon down to the gospels and Paul, perhaps under the influence of the writings of Marcion, and included the Pauline Epistle to the Laodiceans, which is spurious, but no more so than the Pastoral Epistles that are included in our New Testaments.

The Paulicians had much in common with the Marcionites, and they may have been heirs to some late Marcionite communities, or may simply have picked up the principles from a Marcionite commentary and fanned the ashes back into a flame. It is quite likely that there was also some genuine Manichaean influence, and, like subsequent sects such as the Bogomils and Cathars, they were referred to as Manichaeans by orthodox Catholics.

The Paulicians may have had a secret teaching accessible only to their initiates. They did not revere the cross, for they said, in a very Pauline way, that Christ was the cross. It has also been suggested that they may have originated as Adoptionists and become dualists only later. Adoptionist Christology lends itself to being a model for spiritual experience. Adoptionism takes its name from the view that Jesus was adopted as the son of God at some point in his life, and this is clearly very different from the view that he was God incarnate from birth. Adoptionist Christologies usually take the view that Jesus was adopted as the son of God either when he was baptized by John (when the dove came down and a voice from heaven was heard) or else that he was adopted on the cross.

Paul wrote that we are all sons of God. The spirit descends on someone who is adopted by God, and so becomes a child of God. This is equivalent to experiencing the Holy Spirit, which is gnosis. So if the Paulicians were Adoptionist and dualist they were surely Gnostics.

The Byzantine Christians were convinced that the Paulicians took their inspiration from the Manichaeans, even if modern scholars are not so sure. Peter of Sicily, a Byzantine writer, explained the origin of Paulicianism as being the result of a Manichaean woman, Callinice, bringing up her two sons in the 'heresy' and gaining followers in eastern Anatolia. This origin story is rejected as legend by most modern commentators, such as Yuri Storyanov, who places more importance on the influence of Constantine of Mananalis in the seventh century, who was the first Paulician religious leader, or *didaskalos*.

The Paulicians spread through Armenia and Asia Minor and even had a diocese in Corinth, where Paul had founded the Church in the first century. They were badly treated until the Iconoclast movement won state support in Byzantium and the Paulicians allied themselves with the Iconoclasts. But when the Iconoclasts lost influence the Paulicians were persecuted once again, and a succession of wars and persecutions diminished their influence. Unusually for Gnostics, the Paulicians had a warlike strain to them, and in the First Crusade, Paulician units fought for the side of Islam.

In the tenth century some Paulicians were resettled in Thrace – modern Bulgaria – which had been devastated by plague and needed to be repopulated. The last Paulician was said to have been converted to Catholicism in Bulgaria in the seventeenth century, but the sect's influence had been inconsiderable for centuries. Paulician teachings influenced the folklore of Bulgaria, which has dualist aspects to it, and the deportation of Paulicians into Thrace more than likely helped the dualist teachings to survive and be transmitted to the Bogomils.

* * *

The Bogomils were the original buggers, not because they had a predilection for male homosexuality or sex with animals, but because Bogamil is the etymological basis for the word 'bugger'. The Bogomils were called Bulgarians after their country of origin; Bulgarian became 'bugger', which then became a synonym first for any heretic and then for a sodomite.

They were already widespread in Bulgaria by the middle of the tenth century. Despite being so close to Constantinople, the centre of Byzantine Christianity, Bulgaria and the Balkans in general had preserved their pagan religion for an extended period. Pagan mystery religions, central Asian sects and even Dionysian cults are attested in the Bulgarian Empire in the seventh century and later.

In the tenth century, Paulicians were resettled in Thrace. Byzantine Orthodox Christianity also had a certain strength in the Eastern Balkans, but could not assume a dominant position. Thus the area was a hotbed of pagan and heretical Christian sects. When the Bulgarian Empire collapsed in the fourteenth century, Bogomilism collapsed with it, though the very last Bogomils were recorded in Bosnia in 1867.[67]

The Bogomils are named after their legendary founder Bogomil, which means priest or father in Bulgarian. In Bogomil myth and cosmogony, the angel Satanel wished to rule the disorganized lower levels of the universe and led a revolt against God. In doing so, Satanel was stripped of the 'el' suffix to his name and thus became Satan. The parable of the unjust steward or steward of unrighteousness in Luke was interpreted by the Bogomils as referring to Satan. In a complex cosmology, there are seven heavens beyond the sky, and seven more that are ruled by Satan.

As with the Paulicians and the Cathars, there is a demiurge who is identified with Satan. In at least one source, the devil is identified with the God of the Old Testament which, as we have seen so many times, is a classic feature of Gnostic Christian dualism. Some Bogomils considered both Jesus and the devil to be sons of God and therefore brothers. Like earlier Gnostics, the Bogomils made use of the myth of Eden, but their interpretation is unlike any other. Sathanus' spit becomes a snake that is hidden in the middle of a hollow straw, and this straw takes the place of the tree of good and evil, so, in a completely original twist, both the tree and the snake are the demiurge! Sathanus seduces Eve and thus gives rise to a demonic human race.

No higher aeon or spiritual power has any place in the Eden myth of the Bogomils, all is the result of the demiurge's tricks, and so Adam and Eve have little choice but to be ensnared by him. Satan created the trap and sprang it. Once again, it is the demiurge who puts the soul into the body, but he is forced (in some versions of the myth) to accept some of the higher God's influence.

In some Gnostic and other unorthodox traditions, Enoch,

who like Seth receives only the sketchiest treatments in Genesis, was the revealer figure. But the Bogomils practised the ultimate in inverse exegesis (inverting the inversion) and turned an esoteric hero into the mouthpiece of the demiurge. The Bogomil Enoch teaches and promotes the religion of the demiurge. God prepares to send Jesus as a remedy for Enoch's misleading scriptures, which teach the practices of external religion. In response, Sathanus gives Moses the Torah, sends him over the Red Sea. He also gives him three pieces of wood with which to construct Jesus' cross. Time is treated in an intriguing fashion here, with a single celestial event (the preparation of Jesus) being connected to an earthly history that spans hundreds of years.

Once Jesus does manifest on Earth he has no physical body, but he is a spirit. The demiurge or archon sends his angel, Elias, as John the Baptist, who opposes Jesus and is associated with the conventional Church and its sacraments. The overall emphasis of the myth is the contrast between the true God and the false demiurge, and on the Bogomils as the upholders of true religion against the false demiurgic religion of the Catholics and Orthodox Christians.

The Bogomils, or at least the inner elect circle, were encratic, foregoing sex, wine and indulgent foods. There were Bogomils in Bosnia and the Bosnian bishop Niketas attended the grand Cathar council in 1107. Thus there were Gnostic dualists as far east as Bulgaria and as far west as France during the medieval period. The connection between the Bosnian Church and the Bogomils is somewhat disputed, but there were rumours of a mysterious Bogomil anti-pope in Croatia. The Bosnians rejected much of the Old Testament, believing that the patriarchs and prophets were devils and that the souls of men were fallen demons, who could return to heaven after they had 'made penance' in one or more bodies, that is, the soul had been incarnated in various bodies.[68]

* * *

So the slender thread of dualism runs from the ancient Gnostics to the Manichaeans to the Paulicians to the Bogomils and finally to the Cathars. But it is the far more variegated influences of Kabbalah, Neoplatonism, Islamic Gnosis and Sufism — none of them quite identical to Gnosticism, but each of them having strong similarities — that kept gnosis alive.

CHAPTER 9

THE GOOD CHRISTIANS: THE CATHARS

The Cathars have attracted a considerable amount of attention recently, both in a historical context and in connection to such controversial material as the Rennes-le-Château mysteries. Historical sites connected with the Cathars, such as Montségur, have become tourist spots; but the interest in the Cathars is usually in their tragic and dramatic story rather than their beliefs; in their downfall rather than in their success.

Our historical knowledge of ancient Gnostic groups is very patchy, but we now have an excellent range of Gnostic texts. The situation with the Cathars is the reverse. The tragic tale of their history is well documented in contemporary chronicles and in the records of the Inquisition, but their writings and their beliefs are little known and do not survive in quantity, so many modern accounts only vaguely mention their beliefs, such as reincarnation, and their vegetarianism. We still only have a few pieces of Bogomil and Cathar scripture and of all the possible treasures that the Cathars are rumoured to have deposited in Montségur or Rennes-le-Château or in numerous other places in the

Languedoc, surely the most exciting and useful would be a cache of the Cathars' own writings, perhaps discovered in the style of Nag Hammadi or the Dead Sea Scrolls by some Languedocian shepherd.

In this chapter I will concentrate on the beliefs of the Cathars, on what might make them Gnostic, or on what they have in common with the earlier Gnostics. As I mentioned in the introduction, Gnosticism is best treated as a web of related beliefs, attitudes, practices and approaches to the spiritual development of mankind in the world.

According to Gnostics, the world is fallen, imperfect and evil, the creation of an ignorant lower God. But mankind contains a spark from the higher, eternal God, and that spark can be developed through Gnosis. Therein salvation lies. Hence, there are two powers, and so Gnostics are dualist, pitting the higher God against the God of this world and pitting the body against the spirit. Gnosticism is usually, but not uniquely, Christian, since the figure of Christ usually has a role in the myths, and Gnostics have a particular view of the Bible that involves either allegory or an inversion of the orthodox interpretation. Not all of the above criteria are true for any particular example of Gnosticism, but many of the above are true for the Cathars.

Like the Manichaeans, Paulicians and Bogomils, the Cathars were dualists. For the Cathars, salvation seems to have been achieved mainly through the administration of the consola-mentum rite, and the subsequent moral and ritual obligations that attended it. But there are indications that this rite itself may have been accompanied by gnosis and may have been perceived as conferring a spiritual experience as the Cathar received it.

Like the Manichaeans, the Cathars were divided into two classes, the Believers and the Perfect.

The Cathars had close relations with the Bogomils, from whom they may have originated, but Manichaean expert Edward de Buhn has suggested that the Cathar religion might initially have been the result of a Manichaean cell going underground to such an extent that in a couple of generations it was transformed into the Christian Cathars. Whether this was the case or not, Cathars were known to many as Manichaeans, or 'Manichees' – a standard insult for any group perceived as heretical.

The Catholics also called them Cathars or Albigensians as a way of divorcing them from the Christian brotherhood, and making them different. They were known as Piphles in Flanders, and as Texerant in the rest of France (which didn't include the Languedoc at that time), from a word for 'weaver'. The occupation of weaver was considered unclean and was thus forbidden to the clergy, and was associated with witchcraft and heresy.[69]

To the Catholics, Cathars were heretics. To the corrupt, venal clergy of the Catholic Church they were simply competition sent by the devil; to the more sincere and spiritual members of that Church they were still heretics, yet also an indication of how the Church needed to remind itself of its duty, and an incentive for reform. To the Cathars the reverse was true: the Catholic Church was the Church of the devil, and the Cathars felt that they were continuing the genuine tradition of the apostles.

Ironically, it is a heresiologist who provided the best-known and most laudatory definition of the name Cathar as 'pure ones' or the Pure. For a long time, scholars followed the derivation of 'Cathar' proposed by Eckbert of Schönau, who wrote 13 sermons, *Sermones contra Catharos*, in 1163, the same year in which the Council of Tours passed legislation against the Albigensians. He derived Cathar from the Greek *katharos*, meaning 'pure ones'. An earlier heretical group named the Katharoi were mentioned in the Council of Nicea, but they are unrelated to the medieval Cathars. However, the term 'Cathar is now taken as a twelfth-century German play on words implying a cat worshipper.'[70] The cat reference comes from a tradition that the Cathars, like other heretics, supposedly performed a rite which involved kissing a cat's backside. Medieval Christian heresy hunters seem to have had a fascination with the 'foul kiss' in its various forms.

Until the present day they were perhaps more commonly known as the Albigensians, from the town of Albi in the Languedoc, which was the place first recognized as being a hotbed of Catharism. The Cathars were content merely to call themselves 'good Christians' and resisted the etymological jibes of the Catholics.

Cathars existed both in southern France and in Italy and in small groups further afield in northern Europe, perhaps even in England, but our knowledge of the history of the Cathars in the French Languedoc region is far superior because they were the subject of such attention as the victims of the Albigensian crusade and the Inquisition.

The historical setting for the Cathars was very different to that of the ancient Gnostics, the backdrop being high medieval Europe: the France and Italy of late romance. Medieval Europe was a fascinating dichotomy, it was a sudden spring, the new birth of culture, swiftly followed by winter and the murderous hand of plague and Inquisition. The crusades combined both of these elements in one, fusing the naivety and valour and enthusiasm of the emergent Western Christendom with the religious intolerance and murderous barbarism that characterized medieval Europe at its worst. High culture and sincere spirituality existed side by side with dogmatic slaughter and greed.

Our first certain historical indication of the existence of the Cathars sets the scene for the rest of their history. We first come across them in a letter from Eberwin, a prior based near Cologne, who wrote to the great Cistercian saint and reformer, Bernard of Clairvaux (1090–1153), that heretics had been discovered in the area. In the same year, similar heretics were discovered in Bonn. Those heretics who did not escape from the Church authorities were faced with the decision to recant their heretical teaching and rejoin the Church of Rome, or to burn.

The Catholic Bernard of Clairvaux was a conflicted man: spiritual but intolerant, strict and austere – an ascetic who was so hard on his body that he was said to have smelled constantly of vomit – but in many ways he was an enlightened and spiritual man. His commentary on the Song of Songs used the allegorical method in abundance, interpreting the poem as referring to the relationship between man and God, and his reverence for the Virgin Mary reintroduced a feminine element into Catholic Christianity. But his loyalty to the papacy was unswerving and he had no tolerance for any doctrine that contradicted the Catholic doctrine – and Cathar doctrine was strongly in conflict with the Catholic.

Bernard was one of a number of otherwise admirable medieval spiritual figures who was anti-Cathar. Figures such as Hildegard of Bingen, the formidable abbess who composed such beautiful music, who, in 1163, had an apocalyptic dream in which the emergence of the Cathars represented the release of

Satan from the bottomless pit of John's revelation; and Dante, who while he did not explicitly attack the Cathars, praised some of the personages who aided the Albigensian Crusade that was to decimate the Cathars of the Languedoc. Dante admired St Dominic (*Paradiso* XII:1) or Domingo de Guzmán (1170–1221), who preached against the Cathars and was a close friend of Simon de Montfort, and also Fulk or Folquet of Marseilles (*Paradiso* IX:37) (1155–1231), a troubadour turned Cistercian who was a leader in the Albigensian Crusade.

Paradoxically, the medieval Church could foster these great spiritual figures at a time when the Church itself was so involved in temporal matters and its clergy was so corrupt. In contrast, the Cathars were not known for great and unique individual artists or thinkers, but for the piety and simplicity of so many of their rank and file members. Bernard famously called the Cathars 'foxes in the vineyard of the Lord', referring to Song of Songs 2:15. But Bernard thought that it was the tongue, not the sword, that could best root out the Cathar heresy.

In 1145, Bernard visited the Languedoc, beginning with Albi, to preach against heretics (not only Cathars) and later to dispute publicly with them. He was seemingly successful in Albi, but in the village of Verfeil near Toulouse his preaching was drowned out by the noise of knights clashing their armour with their swords. They were probably not Cathars, but local landowners with a strong anti-clerical bent. The Languedoc was home not only to heretics but to strong-willed noblemen with an anti-ecclesiastical bias who were eager to limit the influence of Rome in their region.

* * *

The history of the Cathars is well documented after the Cologne and Bonn heretic incidents, but it is history told by the winners, and thus is presented as the history of heretics. But what did the Cathars actually believe? What ideas and practices so threatened the Catholic Church?

Cathars held a wide variety of beliefs and there was no central body to govern and approve dogma. Much of our information comes from the final period of Catharism, from Inquisition interrogations, at a time when the beliefs had quite likely changed in response to the persecution. We cannot necessarily retroject fourteenth-century beliefs into the thirteenth century, or assume that a view said to be held by Italian Cathars was also held by French Cathars in the Languedoc. Indeed, for much, if not most, of the material we are indebted to the enemies of the Cathars, who held that the doctrines of their opponents were by definition false, and may have exaggerated or fabricated certain elements. Yet in the following overview of Cathar thought and practice I shall not for the most part attempt to distinguish the various strands of tradition, but merely give a taste of the thought and ritual of the Cathars. In Gnosticism, diversity, not dogma, is the norm.

There are examples of both absolute dualism and mitigated dualism in Catharism. There is a clear distinction between absolute or radical dualism, in which the entire universe has from the beginning been governed by two powers – one dark and one light – and mitigated or moderate dualism, which posits a good God or good force at the beginning and culmination, at the highest point of the universe, but which acknowledges that an independent evil force or lower God has as much, or more, influence on our present world. The Sethians and Valentinians were mitigated dualists, the Manichaeans absolute dualists.

It is easy enough for either version of dualism to be transmuted into the other. The temporary status of mitigated dualism may be seen as a single example of the absolute unending battle between good and evil, and absolute dualism may be converted into moderate dualism by deciding that the unending playoff of absolute dualism has been set up by a higher power than the current lords of light and darkness.

The Cathars did not posit a previously unknown lower God as the creator of our world but, like the Paulicians and Bogomils, thought that Lucifer or Satan was the lower God that opposed the Good God. According to the mitigated dualist view, Satan fell from heaven, but according to the absolutist view, he is, if not equal with God, at least as eternal and unending as God.

Cathars believed that the soul would go through many lifetimes before it achieved salvation. Some thought that the final lifetime of a Cathar Perfect would always be male, but this is only attested in late belief. The importance of reincarnation was that it gave the soul repeated attempts at attaining freedom from this world and hence salvation and a return to the true God. According to the Cathars, the soul transmigrates from one body to another, including animal bodies. One Cathar recalled that in his previous incarnation he was the horse of a local lord. In response to a nagging memory he had of a previous lifetime, he searched between two rocks and found a horseshoe that he remembered shedding during his previous life as a horse.[71]

A Cathar who died as a Perfect would attain salvation and be freed from having to transmigrate into another body. A Cathar who died with the status of Believer would have to wait for a future life in which she or he would become a Perfect and would die with that status intact.

The Cathars' belief in reincarnation has had a peculiar resonance in the accounts of modern people who believe that they have been Cathars in a previous life. Arthur Guirdham's *The Cathars and Reincarnation* recounts the story of a young Englishwoman who seemed to recall her previous life as a thirteenth-century French Cathar in seemingly convincing detail. Cathars vie with ancient Egyptians and Tibetans as the most popular subjects of past life regression.

As in other forms of Gnosticism, Docetism, the view that Jesus did not have a physical body and never had a substantial flesh and blood existence, crops up time and again in Cathar thought. Some Cathars believed that Christ was an angel and his body was a phantasm, neither suffering nor dying nor rising again.[72] Some thought that Mary was an angel too. Others thought, like the Bogomils, that the spiritual Jesus had come into this world through his mother as if she were merely a conduit, and that she contributed nothing at all to his earthly character or existence. Some Italian Cathars believed that Mary, Jesus and John the Evangelist had all three been angels and were given human form. Yet other Italian Cathars believed that Jesus had a fleshly body but discarded it during his ascension.[73]

The Cathars consisted of two classes, the Believers and the Perfect. Those who were not Cathars but were interested in their doctrines and respected them were called Listeners. 'Perfect' may actually have originated as a term used sarcastically by their enemies. Because so much of our knowledge comes from the pens of the Cathars' enemies, we cannot be certain that this was their own name for themselves. The Perfect were the inner circle of the Cathars, the true Cathars who had dedicated themselves to the vows of purity, which included ascetic practices such as not eating meat, particularly red meat, abstaining from sex, lying and swearing oaths. It seems that only Perfects were fully initiated into the dualist teaching and mythology and into the inner meaning of their scriptures and practices. This is another indication that the Cathars might have been genuinely Gnostic: knowledge of the situation of mankind in the universe was essential to salvation.

* * *

The medieval Catholic attitude to women was famously oppressive. Certainly there were exceptions in strong women like the Cathar-hating Abbess Hildegard of Bingen, whose music has only truly been appreciated in our generation. Women were adored in the secular poetry of the Troubadours and in the charming culture of courtly love, but were irrelevant to the Church. Bernard of Clairvaux detested the sexual attractiveness of women, and found the struggle against his desire for them difficult, complaining that 'to be always with a woman and not have intercourse with her is more difficult than to raise the dead.'[74] Yet he was responsible for bolstering the importance of the Virgin Mary cult, which Stephen O'Shea called 'a bone thrown to the metaphysically dispossessed.'

Medieval Catholic clergymen had become notorious for their inability to keep to their vows of celibacy. Today, priests who molest children or indulge themselves with members of their congregation regularly make the headlines, but they are not nearly so numerous in proportion to the population as were their medieval equivalents, nor were today's whistle-blowing possibilities available to the earlier victims. The contrast between the official Church and Cathars and other heretics is well illustrated by the following anecdote.

Gervase of Tilbury, a Catholic nobleman, was out riding with the Archbishop of Rheims and other members of the clergy, when they met a pretty, unaccompanied peasant girl. Gervase admired her beauty, spoke to her pleasantly for a while and tried to convince her of the delights of having sex with him. She declined his advances and protested that she was a virgin. Rather than accept this at face value, he interpreted this as a heretical belief that she did not wish to corrupt her body. When the Archbishop, who was nearby, was informed of this, he was appalled. Not by Gervase's advances towards the innocent girl, but by her refusal to submit herself to him. She was arrested, interrogated, refused to recant and was burnt to death.[75]

The traditions of the Languedoc region certainly helped the Cathars to grant greater importance to women than was typical of the medieval Catholic Church. Marriage was not particularly important to the Cathars, and in the Languedoc legacies were split evenly between all surviving children, regardless of their sex or primacy, so daughters could inherit their parents' wealth. In addition there was generally no gender restriction on becoming a Perfect although it was common for women to become Perfects later in life than men, and they usually waited until they had fulfilled their child-rearing and mothering duties. Female Perfects, the Good Women (or 'fair heretics' as one Troubadour named them,[76] tended not to travel as much as men, instead establishing communal homes in which the better-off Cathar girls and young women could be brought up and educated.

Still, not all Cathar references to women were complimentary. According to some female Believers interviewed by the Inquisition in the fourteenth century, women were blamed for encouraging creation via their sexual attractiveness and for replaying the role of Eve. The Church of Rome was called 'the harlot of the apocalypse', which is hardly complimentary to women, and women only made up around a third of the Cathar population. A French Cathar expert, Jean Duvernoy, calculated that around 30 per cent of Believers were female. Interestingly, 34 per cent of Perfects were female, indicating that female Believers were slightly more likely to become part of the Cathar elite and to receive the consolamentum than males were. But this is still quite a contrast to the Catholic system, in which no woman could ever become a priest.

A Believer was converted into a Perfect by the consolamentum rite. The consolamentum was 'baptism, confirmation, ordination, and, if received at death's door, extreme unction all rolled into one.'[77] It granted salvation but demanded great responsibility and was very different from the rites that were slanderously attributed to the Cathars, such as the kissing of a cat's anus.

During the consolamentum, some Cathars held that the *spiritus paraclitum*, the comforting or consoling spirit (as in the paraclete in the Gospel of John 14:16, 26) was sent down to the Believer who was becoming a Perfect.[78] This paraclete designates the spirit for each soul-angel trapped in matter. Here we have arrived again at a typically Gnostic view of the soul and spirit, with the spirit being the transcendent and divine aspect of a person. In the mysterious passage in the Gospel of John, Jesus promises to send the paraclete, a Greek word which may be translated as advocate or comforter, or consoler. It is the Latin equivalent of the paraclete that gives us the term consolamentum.

The paraclete was important to Mani too, and Mani's heavenly twin or divine self was called the paraclete. Thus the rite of the consolamentum was an initiation into the life of the spirit. Many aspects of Cathar organization and practice strongly resemble Manichaeism, so the standard labelling of Cathars as 'Manichees' was by no means inaccurate. The Manichaeans were also divided into two groups, Hearers and Perfect or Elect, and the Manichaean Perfect were under similar restrictions to the Cathar Perfect – celibacy, vegetarianism, not lying.

The transubstantiation of bread and wine in the Catholic Eucharist was laughed at by Cathars. Peter Autier, the fourteenth-century Perfect who led a Cathar revival, commented that 'if Christ's body had been as big as Mt Bugarach [1,200m/4,00ft] it would still have been consumed long ago by all those priests' mouths.' It is an argument that would not be out of place in the writings of Richard Dawkins.[79]

The efficacy of the consolamentum depended on the continuing sinlessness of the Perfect who had given the rite. If this Perfect failed to keep the obligations of the consolamentum, then all of the Perfect initiated by him would lose their status as Perfect and all would need to be reinitiated by another Perfect. This scheme must have been extremely inconvenient at times, but it placed the entire burden of purity on the Cathar Perfects themselves. They were responsible for both their own purity and for the purity of others. This was a very different arrangement to, for instance, the Catholic Mass, in which the principle was *ex opere operato, non ex opere operantis*, that grace 'results from what is performed, not who performs it'. Mass performed by a corrupt or sinful Catholic priest is still valid.

Thus both the Cathar elite and the ordinary Believers were bound by voluntary ties. The Believers gave a greeting called the melioramentum to the Perfect and received a blessing in return;

the Perfect had to keep to their vows or risk losing their status and reducing to the status of Believers the Perfect that they had inducted. And the Believers were not merely bowing to authority when they greeted Perfects with the melioramentum but were making a voluntary acknowledgment of the importance of the Perfects.

Believers often became Perfects at the end of their lives, particularly during the periods when Cathars had to practise their faith in total secrecy and when the Cathar faith itself was being strongly persecuted; during these times the position of the Cathars resembled that of the Jews in Nazi Germany.

* * *

The most controversial Cathar practice was the endura. This might be considered as being halfway between a hunger strike and euthanasia. Once the endura had been declared, the Cathar receiving it would fast until death came. The endura allowed Cathars to choose a noble death over the tortures of the Inquisition and the rite became most important during the later stages of Catharism when Believers and Perfects alike lived continually under the shadow of persecution. By that stage it was often performed at the same time as the consolamentum on a Cathar Believer who was close to death. This ensured that the Believer would become a Perfect and would remain so until the advent of death.

Many Cathars used it to die with dignity when in the extremes of illness, or to die secure in their faith rather than be burnt as heretics or interrogated and forced to recant. Occasionally an extremely ill Cathar would recover unexpectedly after having received the endura. One woman kept the endura for 12 weeks before dying. And at least one Cathar abandoned the endura fast when his health began to improve and continued as a Cathar despite having broken his fast.

Cathars were forbidden to swear oaths. This might seem trivial from a modern point of view, but the entire feudal system was based on the swearing of oaths.[80] The Church provided the mechanism for swearing oaths and thus was an important middle man in all aspects of business. A refusal to swear oaths cut out the middle man and any contract would be between one person and another with God alone as witness. In refusing to swear oaths the Cathars were subverting the temporal power of the medieval Church, giving yet another example of their willingness to take the responsibility for their lives onto themselves.

The Cathars placed more importance on the canonical Gospel of John than on any other text. As we have seen, the Gospel of John has some Gnostic features that may be the result of a Gnostic influence, or of a proto-Gnosticism, or of a kind of anti-Gnosticism – an appropriation by proto-Orthodoxy of the more acceptable Gnostic themes. The figure of Satan has acquired greater significance in the Gospel of John than in the synoptic gospels, and the Cathars interpreted Satan as being the demiurge. The Gospel of John could fuel their dualistic outlook in a way that the synoptic gospels could not. There is even a very slight possibility that the *Gospel of Thomas* was still circulating at that time for a saying from Thomas is also found in a medieval Italian gospel harmony.

In 1167, Cathars from the Languedoc, from northern France and from Italy gathered in St Felix en Laurgais, a small Languedocian town perched on a rock. Perfects and Believers crowded into the small fortified town, establishing and re-establishing contact with each other. One notable attendant was not a Cathar, but a Bogomil, a mysterious Greek-speaking man named Nicetas who may have been Bishop of Constantinople, who re-administered the consolamentum. The council of St Felix established (or re-established) a strong link between the Cathars and the Bogomils and introduced some unity into the Cathar faith.

At the peak of Catharism there were bishops and a certain amount of ecclesiastical authority, but this level of organization was most likely a necessary response to the challenge of the Catholic Church since it was not fundamental to the Cathars, and for the most part they remained a loose network of devout people in which individual purity and application of their principles and knowledge were paramount.

* * *

We have so far dwelt on the teaching of the Cathars, but it is the bloody tale of their persecution and slaughter that is better known. In *A New Model of the Universe*, the esotericist P.D. Ouspensky looked down from the towers of Notre Dame de Paris, the great cathedral that so well represents the spiritual, esoteric side of the Catholic Church, and pondered that there were two histories in the world:

> 'One history passes by in full view and, strictly speaking, is the *history of crime*, for if there were no crimes there would be no history. All the most important turning-points and stages of this history are marked by crimes: murders, acts of violence, robberies, wars, rebellions, massacres, tortures, executions ... This is one history, the history which everyone knows, the history which is taught in schools.'

And now it is time to turn to the history of crime. In the early thirteenth century, the Languedoc saw many debates between Cathar and Catholic as the Church attempted to convince the laity to side with it. The Cathars knew their New Testament well, and were able debaters. Both sides claimed apostolic succession: the Cathars through the administration of the consolamentum, which they thought could be traced back to the apostles and Mary Magdalene, and the Catholics through the succession of priests and bishops and the pope's claim to inherit the office of St Peter. Neither party acknowledged the validity of the other. The Catholics thought, of course, that the Cathars were heretics, of the devil's party. But the Cathars too threw insults at the Romans, calling them, among other things, a 'Church of wolves' and a 'Church of whores'. The results of these debates were inconclusive, and some of the wavering laity returned to the Church, but the debates were certainly not won conclusively by the Catholics.

The debates failed to uproot the perceived heresy, not only because the Cathars had many attractive qualities, but also because the Catholic priesthood set such a bad example. In the Languedoc the contrast between the Cathar Perfect and the Roman priests and bishops was startling. The Cathars were pious, poor, simple and sincere. The Catholic priests were decadent and venal and abused their positions. There were movements toward reform within the Catholic Church, and the lifetime of Francis of Assissi overlapped with the existence of the Cathars. But it was St Dominic, founder of the Dominicans, who actively fought against Catharism.

Dominic was as ascetic as the most extreme Perfect, and dedicated himself to the putting down of heresy. His behaviour set an inspiring counter-example, but his conversions amounted only to a few dozen in the space of several years. It was a secular, worldly element that finally put the Cathars on the defensive. The Dominicans' greatest bequest to civilization was the notorious Inquisition. The Inquisition was founded in 1229, 20 years after the Albigensian Crusade began, specifically to root out Cathars, but also to attack heresy in general, wherever in Christendom it may be found.

* * *

The crusade that was to finally wipe out the Cathars was triggered in January 1208 when Peter of Castelnau, a Cistercian monk and the Pope's legate, who had been in the Languedoc on matters connected with heresy (attempting to persuade a renegade feudal lord, Raymond VI, Count of Toulouse), left for Rome. Talks had broken down and there was much acrimony. Scarcely a day into his trip back to Rome, Peter of Castelnau was attacked by an unknown rider and murdered by sword. This violence was peripheral to the lives of the peace-loving Cathar Perfects, but it prompted the Albigensian Crusades, which were to prove the turning point in the fortune of the Cathars.

A crusade is a holy war, a military campaign that promotes the cross and the Church. The popular and historical conceptions of the crusades have long since moved away from the glorious image of virtuous Christians fighting against the heathen Muslims, macho semi-saints, their chain-mail glittering in the Palestinian sun, as the red crosses on white banners are caught by the breeze. The crusades are now acknowledged as being largely sordid in their action and were the epitome of masculine medieval violence.

The Albigensian Crusade began in 1209, set in motion by a

papal bull from Innocent III after the debates and disputes between Cathar and Catholic had little success in turning the Languedocians away from the dualist faith. Unlike the other crusades, which directed the aggression of Europe outwards, towards the near East, the Albigensian Crusade, also known as the Cathar Wars, was a fight between north and south. As well as being a religious war, it also amounted to a civil war. France did not yet exist as an entity, but the northern part was already known as France, from the northern Frankish people who had conquered it. The victory of the Catholic northerners resulted in the entire province being incorporated into the Kingdom of France.

In 1209, around 10,000 crusaders had massed in Lyon, fighting for the noble causes of hard cash, an easing of their debts, and the remission of sins to boot. They first attacked Béziers, sparing Montpellier which was not sympathetic to Catharism. Cathar historian Stephen O'Shea called the sack of Béziers 'the Guernica of the Middle Ages.'[81] This is where the monk Arnold Amaury commaded the crusaders to spare no one, with the extraordinarily cynical comment: 'Kill them all, God will know his own.'[82]

The town was left open to the onslaught of the crusaders when some Béziers youths opened a gate to attack a single crusader who had been taunting the townspeople from a bridge, and the noble crusaders 'left not one who pisseth against a wall'. Around 20,000 inhabitants were slaughtered on 22 July 1209, ironically, the feast day of Mary Magdalene.

Carcasonne was the next town to be taken – this time it lasted through a genuine medieval siege until the water was cut off and the townspeople were expelled, naked. Carcasonne was given to Simon de Montfort, a brave but bloodthirsty and unprincipled knight who emerged as the champion of the crusaders. As the year went on, Albi, after which both the crusade and the Cathars were named, fell, then town after town were taken in siege after siege, slaughter after slaughter.

> 'The Lastours castles held out as a centre of opposition to the conquests of Simon de Montfort, who determined to wipe them out. In this, he was bound to fail, having to launch simultaneous attacks on three castles protected by sheer rockfaces and defended by a nobleman who, though not a Cathar, was aware of the importance of the campaign de Montfort was waging against his *suzerain*, the viscount of Carcassonne. De Montfort decided against attacking the castles and instead resorted to a cruel ploy that typifies the barbarity of this war. He brought prisoners from the village of Bram and had their eyes gouged out and their ears, noses and lips cut off. One prisoner, left with a single good eye, led them to Lastours as a warning. The ploy failed; the castles put up more resistance and held out until the supposedly impregnable fortress at Termes fell in November 1210. The lord of Cabaret then surrendered.'[83]

After the initial successes, the progress of the crusaders slowed a little. Feudal political issues developed, and there were reversals and some Languedocian towns and fortresses threw off their northern invaders. Toulouse was captured by the northern crusaders and then retaken by the southern forces. Simon de Montfort was killed in 1218 trying to retake Toulouse. Cathars were killed, their land was taken, and some Cathar Believers fought on behalf of the southern forces. But for the most part, the Albigensian Crusade had little to do with the beliefs or principles of the Cathars and everything to do with temporal power, with the workings of the fallen world crafted and controlled by the demiurge, Lucifer. But all of this was 'the history of crime'.

* * *

Montségur, a citadel high in the Pyrenees, was by no means the bloodiest massacre of Cathars, nor was it the longest siege or the most intense period of military campaigning. But it became the most famous. Laurence Durrell was not far wrong when, in a preface to Lacarriere's book *The Gnostics*, he called it 'that Thermopylae of the Gnostic soul.'[84]

The citadel of Montségur had become a real Cathar community. All who lived there were either Believers or else sympathetic to the Cathars. Around 200 Perfect lived in the area, and it was the largest Cathar community of the thirteenth century. The siege lasted for ten months: the circumference of the mountain base was 2 miles/3km long and the mountain citadel was extremely difficult to take. By the end of the year 1243, some mountaineers from Gascony had successfully taken a neighbouring peak and were able to use this as a point of attack. On 2 March 1244, Montségur surrendered. The Cathars were given terms that seemed soft in comparison with the slaughters and cheated promises of the previous sieges and battles. As long as they submitted to the Inquisition and renounced Catharism they would be spared. But this was a ploy by the conquerors who wished to appear merciful; they knew that none of the Perfect were likely to renounce their faith. And, as they expected, none did so. In fact another 21 Believers opted to receive the consolamentum, to become Perfect and burn with the other 200. It was not the extremity of the bloodshed or the quantity of the slaughtered that distinguished the massacre of Montségur, but the nobility of its martyrs.

* * *

Yet Catharism was not a centralized religion. All that was needed was for a single Perfect to survive, and from him or her a Cathar network could grow: a single spark was all that was needed to reignite the flames. Around the turn of the fourteenth century, Peter Autier and his brother William led a revival in the Languedoc. Peter had travelled to Italy where he had been trained in Cathar ways by Italian Cathars and had received the consolamentum. He and his brother converted a few dozen volunteers to Catharism, and by the end of the first decade, around 1,000 families in the Languedoc practised Catharism in absolute secrecy.

Because of the danger of the Inquisition, Cathars had to hide their loyalties. The importance of the consolamentum increased, while there must have been a certain amount of relaxing of the particular vows that Perfects upheld. Cathar Perfects might make the gesture of the crucifix (whilst mentally intoning 'Here is the forehead, and here is the beard, and here is one ear, and here is the other'), eat meat or even have sex. Perfects went to great lengths to administer the consolamentum secretly to Believers who were about to die. Rather than receive the consolamentum, survive the illness and be unable to keep the terms of the rite, many Believers subsequently took the endura and starved themselves to death.

The Autier network of Cathars was eventually betrayed to the Inquisition by a Believer who was peeved at being refused a loan by another Believer. Peter Autier was burned to death in 1310, and his last request, to preach to the audience, was denied. The last Perfect in the Languedoc was William Bélibaste, a reformed murderer who had a cache of Believers but never initiated a Perfect himself. Urged to leave the Languedoc, he stayed and was burned to death in 1321.

* * *

Were the Cathars really Gnostics? Did they feel that it was knowledge – knowledge of their situation in the world and direct knowledge of God – that brought about their salvation? Certainly their dualism, their belief in a demiurge, emphasis on individual responsibility and salvation, and their belief in re-incarnation strongly resemble Gnostic doctrine. And the connection between the Bogomils and the Cathars arguably gives them a historical lineage that stretches back to the original Gnostics. The reception of the consolamentum placed strong moral and ritual obligations on the receiver, and was a condition for them to receive the full Cathar teaching.

But did the consolamentum also provide initiation into a spiritual world, a world in which one could know the divine directly in this life? The word Perfect also means complete so perhaps the figurative descent of the spirit to join the soul when the consolamentum took place was accompanied then and afterwards by a direct personal experience of the spirit. It is difficult to know, and the surviving documentation and literature do not allow us to tell whether the Cathars were truly Gnostic; but if not, they were certainly the Good Christians.

Although the Cathars would surely have been content to be

remembered by their good works, by their simple lives and their dedication to the true God rather than to Satan and his world, they are instead remembered because they were suppressed and slaughtered. This world truly was a hell, and they were burnt by the Church of Satan. But hopefully their spirits escaped and were united with the good God, and if they weren't, then at least they had the chance to die as Perfects the next time around.

CHAPTER 10

THE LAST GNOSTICS: THE MANDAEANS

The Mandaeans are the last of the ancient Gnostics, the final tributary of a river that has elsewhere dried up or been dammed. Of course, the Mandaeans are not the last to experience gnosis or the last to use Gnostic ideas. Now that the pattern of Gnosticism has been introduced into the world there can always be Gnostics. And where there is gnosis, there is Gnosticism. But the Mandaeans are the last group that has a historical continuity that goes back to the period of classical Gnosticism.

There is much that is startling in the history and mythology of the Mandaeans. Even in the modern climate of historical scepticism, in which the foundation myths of religions, even of the Christian religion, are not taken very seriously, most experts acknowledge that the modern Mandaeans partake of an uninterrupted tradition that stretches back at least to the second century, and perhaps even to the first; their lineage may genuinely stretch back to John the Baptist.

The Mandaeans survived in Iraq and Iran. Despite Islam's current reputation for fundamentalism, the Islamic countries have typically allowed much more religious diversity than the

Christian West. Small sects like the Mandaeans or the Yezidis have survived more or less intact for centuries, despite periodic persecution. That both the Mandaeans and Yezidis have suffered recent persecution and slaughter is in fact a side effect of the twenty-first-century Western intervention in Iraq.

The Mandaeans have survived longer than any other Gnostic group. Time, however, does not favour gnosis (and gnosis is not all that interested in time either). Time loves form, time loves tradition, and traditional formal practices can be passed on from generation to generation in a way that gnosis cannot. Mandaean religion is thus defined more clearly by external factors, such as the emphasis on regular baptism, funerary practices, and considerations of ritual purity.

Although the first Europeans to encounter them often referred to them as St John Christians, the Mandaeans are not Christian. In Muslim society they are called *Subba* or Sabeans and are treated as if they are the mysterious Sabians referred to in the Qur'an, which has in general afforded them greater tolerance as a 'People of the Book' than they would otherwise have received.

They perhaps originated as a baptismal sect echoing other Jewish or Jewish-Christian baptismal sects of the early centuries CE. The name Mandaean derives from the Mandaic word *Manda* meaning knowledge, thus Mandaeans are Gnostics. They have also been called Nazoreans or St John Christians or Johannites, and they have referred to themselves as the elect of righteousness. Many scholars see Mandaeanism as having particularly strong connections with Sethian Gnosticism.

The Mandaeans speak a Semitic language, an East Aramaic dialect that is a close relative of the Aramaic used for the

Babylonian Talmud. They must have encountered the Manichaeans at various times in their history, and some of the Mandaean psalms were adapted by Manichaeans in the third century. There is also a certain amount of overlap between Manichaean and Mandaean myth. Alternative scholarship has suggested that the Mandaeans might have had contact with the Knights Templar, which opens up the possibility of an indirect transmission from the Mandaeans to the Cathars via the Templars.

The Mandaeans are particularly Gnostic in their inversionary treatment of biblical characters, but they develop the inversionary principle in a direction that no other Gnostic movement has taken. In all other Gnostic texts, Jesus is spoken of positively. Jesus may be an aeon, Jesus may be separate from the Christ, and the Christ another aeon, or Jesus may have had no true physical body; he may not have been crucified, may not have suffered, may not physically have been born, may have taken nothing from his birth mother Mary. But, without exception, in Sethian, Valentinian, Thomasine, Manichaean, Bogomil and Cathar texts Jesus plays a positive part in the proceedings. He is the saviour, he is the redeemer, an aeon; he belongs to the Pleroma. The Jewish God was seen as the demiurge, and Moses, as the proponent of the Jewish law, was often reviled in Gnosticism. Peter and the male disciples in general were criticized. But Jesus, never.

For the Christian gospels it was perhaps an 'embarrassment' (a technical term used in scholarship) that Jesus had to be baptized by John, and the importance of John the Baptist diminishes as each gospel writer adapts the story. By the time of the Gospel of John, considered by most scholars to be chronologically the last of the gospels, Jesus suffers John to baptize him, and John protests that he is not worthy to unloose Jesus' sandals. Thus, the Mandaean legends about John and Jesus are truly startling, and truly inversionary in their insistence on presenting Jesus as an inferior figure, a sorcerer and false messiah, as an apostate Mandaean.

For the Mandaeans, the baptism of Jesus presented difficulties in the opposite direction. The problem was not why the superior figure of Jesus should have to submit himself to the ministrations of John, but that John the Baptist should have made such a colossal mistake in agreeing to baptize Jesus at all! According to one Mandaean text, John knew that Jesus was a false prophet and refused to baptize him until Abathur intervened and sent a message telling John to carry it out. The dove that comes down is the Spirit, but not a desirable spirit, it is Ruha, the spirit of darkness.

Mandaeanism is a radical dualism, an eternal opposition of light and dark. Like the Manichaeans, the Mandaeans believed that particles of Light are present in greater quantities in certain substances, and for the Mandaeans the substance filled with the most light is water. All rivers, and even each example of flowing water, are named Jordan in the Mandaean tradition. The Mandaean cosmogony and cosmology is dualistic, with a demiurge and an emanationist; it reinterprets Genesis and has a saviour figure in Manda dHayye, which name means 'Knowledge of Life', that is, gnosis.

The Mandaean world of light is equivalent to the Pleroma of the ancient Gnostics. As in the Manichaean scheme, the world of light is in the north and the world of darkness in the south, and this is almost certainly borrowed from Manichaean mythology. In fact, the Mandaean beliefs are quite a patchwork of material from different traditions. In addition to the Manichaean elements (though the Manichaeans also borrowed from the Mandaeans, namely the Mandaean hymns in the Manichaean psalms) there is the tradition of John the Baptist. A Mandaean presence in first-century Palestine and even a genuine connection to John the Baptist are not unfeasible, but most of the existing Mandaean references to John show every sign of being borrowed from Christian tradition. The baptismal rites have features in common with early Jewish or Jewish-Christian baptismal sects. In addition, the Muslim influence is clear, for the Mandaeans have lived for centuries in countries that are predominantly Muslim. For instance, the name Allah is sometimes used for the Mandaean God.

The Mandaeans are not simply a late hodgepodge of these traditions, but show every sign of being as ancient as Christian Gnosticism. There appears to be no single authoritative account of the Mandaean myth, and this provides another interesting point of comparison with other Gnostics, who also did not have a single definitive version of their myths. Whether or not this is for the same reasons (for example, creativity, lack of centralization, the literary nature of classic Gnostic myth) as the diversity of earlier Gnostic myth is debateable, the comparison remains interesting.

Edmondo Lupieri, a Mandaean scholar, has counted seven different and irreconcilable versions of the creation myth in the Right Ginza, the main compendium of Mandaean myth. Despite having firm practices and a central priesthood, the Mandaeans' beliefs had a flexibility to them.

In Mandaean myth, the ultimate true God is referred to as Life, the First Life, 'the Great Life', the Lord of Greatness, the

Mighty Spirit or the King of Light, or *Mana* ('powerful'). His kingdom, the world of light, is filled with celestial beings known as *uthri* (riches), or *melki* (kings), who continually perform Mandaean rituals in worship of their Lord.

In an emanationist cosmogony, the First Life creates the Second Life, called Yoshamin or Joshamin, and then the Third Life, Abathur, an important character who is the father of the Fourth Life, Ptahil, the creator God. Each of these may be considered a demiurge to some extent, each having a role in the creation of our world. In some versions of the myth, the darkness coexisted with light from the beginning, in the form of the dark water (which might be interpreted as polluted water), from whence arose the lord of darkness, *malka dhshuka*. He is the king of darkness, the lion-headed lord of the dark waters (reminiscent of Ialdabaoth) who self-generates and then emerges from water and creates demons and other evil creatures.

As well as the above version, other myths describe the birth of Ur, a dragon-like monster and lord of darkness, from his mother Ruhā. (In Mandaeanism, the words translated as spirit and soul have the opposite meaning to the rest of Gnosticism. Thus Ruhā (spirit), is the intermediate entity which falls from grace and soul is the eternal, transcendent self.) The evil spirit Ruhā falls from light into darkness and bears Ur, who has the form of a dragon or monster. In the realm of darkness, monsters emerge, evil angels are born, and the malign astrological influences of the Seven – the planets – and the Twelve – the zodiac.

This denigration of astrological influences matches the earlier Gnostic distrust of Heimarmene (fate). Like many other Gnostics, they took astrology seriously but considered the effects of the planets to be malicious. In what seems to have originally been an attempt to avoid the disruptive influence of the stars and planets, Mandaean priests have developed expertise in astrology.

> 'Everything is indicated with exactness according
> to the days and the stars: from when to cut one's
> nails to when to change one's clothes, conduct
> business, travel, convene court cases, request
> favours from the powerful, sow, harvest, hunt,
> catch fish, build a raft, or enter a new house.'[85]

The physical world, Tibil, is created by Ptahil, the Fourth Life, who was following the orders of Abathur, the Third Life. Thus Ptahil is the actual demiurge but he is interpreting the directions of a level higher than himself, not rebelling against divine authority.

The lord of light cannot undo the creation of the world, but he can limit the influence of the darkness. To this end, he sends Manda dHayye, 'knowledge of life', a saviour figure who binds the ruler of darkness and limits his action. There are other saviour figures in Manaeanism, particularly Hibil, Shitil and Anosh — Abel, Seth and Enosh from the Bible, who are once again familiar to us from the ancient Gnostics. Ptahil the demiurge creates Adam from the material of darkness, but Adam is inanimate until his soul Adakas (an abbreviated form of Adam Kasya, 'hidden Adam') arrives from the world of light.

Many of the mythic beings in Manaeanism have fallen from the light or are defined by their earthly existence and yet retain a higher counterpart in the world of light, known as the Dmuta. In later texts even the earth itself has a heavenly counterpart. This is the case with Adam Kasya, who is the heavenly counterpart of the physical Adam. Adam Kasya resides within the earthly or bodily Adam as if within a prison, another example of a Gnostic use of Plato's idea of the body being the prison of the soul. The creation of man is the culmination of the process of creation or begetting or emanation which began with the second life Yoshamin. Adam does not sin and fall, but in a strange and pathetic interpretation, Adam refuses to die when his time has come.

The focus of soteriology in Manaeanism is the liberation of the soul from the body and from this world, and it is Manda dHayye, 'knowledge of life', who gives the saving knowledge to Adam's soul. Thus Gnostic redemption is at the centre of the myth. Manda dHayye, from whom the name Mandaean is derived, reminds Adam of the divine origin of his soul and teaches him about the origin of the world and the various beings and their importance. This is the esoteric core of the Mandaean teaching and it is truly Gnostic. The soul or spirit belongs to the realm of light, clearly the equivalent of the Pleroma in other traditions. (Mandaean literature, being generally quite contradictory, does not differentiate clearly between the soul and the spirit, and it may be that the words are used interchangeably, or in some cases spirit means the intermediate level – usually called soul by other Gnostics, with spirit the highest level.)

Eve, who is named Hawwa, does not have a large part in the Mandaean mythos, but views of her are mainly positive. This is in contradistinction to the role of women in traditional Mandaean society. There are strong taboos on menstruation, and many laws and traditions place women in a definitely subordinate position and perpetuate many practices that have been abandoned by the modern world. Menstruating women are unclean and are segregated, and so are women who have just given birth. Female virginity is prized and prior to marriage the prospective bride's hymen is examined by three other women. Venereal disease can be passed by women to men, but not vice versa. However, in the past, there were a good number of female scribes and manuscript owners, as attested by the scribal traditions given at the colophon at the end of each Mandaean manuscript, which indicates that women could have status and wealth in Mandaean society.

After death, the soul journeys through eight spheres associated with the seven classical planets and Ruhā, which seek to detain the soul in purgatories. This is again a typical Gnostic feature familiar as the ascent of the soul. If the soul succeeds in negotiating these obstacles, the final stage involves being weighed on the balance of Abathur. The soul must prove that it has the correct weight, which must include the weight of the spirit,[86] not that it is as light as a feather, as in the ancient Egyptian judgment. In a detail very reminiscent of the Gnostic or Manichaean *Hymn of the Pearl*, the successful soul is accompanied on its final journey to the realm of light and is given a robe and confronted with its heavenly twin.

There is also a general apocalyptic judgment that occurs at the end of the world and time, when all are either admitted into the realm of light or are cast into the fire or into the Sea of Sūf – the Red Sea or Sea of Reeds of the biblical Exodus. The Exodus story is the subject of inverse exegesis. The Mandaeans say that they were involved in the events of the Exodus, but they side with the Egyptians, and each year they commemorate the Egyptians who died when the Red Sea closed about them.

In a sophisticated development that also echoes the duplicate figures of the Gnostic or Manichaean *Hymn of the Pearl* (prince/older brother, pearl/robe), eternal versions of the fallen figures remain in the realm of light. The planets, stars and constellations of astrology are always denigrated in the core Mandaean religious texts – the seven and the twelve (and sometimes a mysterious five) are malevolent and are sometimes identified with the ancient planetary gods of Mesopotamia. But there are also Mandaean astrological and magical treatises that seem to have come to terms with the influence of the stars and planets and that contain detailed descriptions of astrological types and influences. These are not only the results of popular religion, but Mandaean priests themselves cast horoscopes and made predictions.

The Mandaeans were recognized as People of the Book by the Muslims, and they do indeed have a wealth of scripture. The soul's journey after death is described in the Diwan Abathur, named after the Third Life who weighs the soul. This and other Mandaean texts are illustrated by strange, witchy glyphs and crude but symbolic sigils. The *Ginza*, the treasure or treasure-house, is perhaps the most important sacred book for the Mandaeans. The *Left Ginza* is the smaller of the two components that make up the *Ginza* – the left-hand pages and right-hand pages are actually separate texts – and contains hymns for the dead and other liturgical material, and is concerned also with the ascent of the soul. The *Right Ginza* is a collection of myths of creation, plus other material. *The Book of John* or *Book of the Kings* is a collection of discourses ascribed to John the Baptist.[87] The *Qolasta* collects prayers, hymns and other liturgical material used at the rituals and ceremonies of the Mandaeans, and is also known as the *Canonical Prayer Book* or *Mandaean Liturgies*. There is also a series of scrolls, magical material and a wealth of untranslated texts.

Although they were always a minority group, the Mandaeans were not terribly sensitive of the feelings of other religious groups; neither Jews nor Christians are extolled by the Mandaeans. Abraham, Moses, Jesus and Muhammad were all false prophets. Mandaean texts claimed that Jews had persecuted them in Jerusalem and that in a play on words in the Mandaic language, Jews were abortions, a term that implied an incomplete religion. Moses either worshipped the evil deity Adonai or was a prophet of Ruhā; Jesus was a false prophet and enemy of John the Baptist, and is sometimes referred to as Christ the Roman; and Muhammad was the 'son of the Arab butcher' and 'son of a sorcerer' and was destined for one of the Mandaean purgatories. But the Mandaeans did read the Qur'an, and passages from the Qur'an are even recommended as part of a healing spell.[88]

These polemics are typical of religions. In a late section of the Talmud a character that is supposed by many scholars to be Jesus is boiled in shit, and in Dante's *Inferno*, Muhammad is placed in the hell of the schismatics and split from groin to neck in imitation of his supposed offence.

* * *

Perhaps gnosis is no longer prevalent among the Mandaeans, but they still represent a genuine stream of tradition. It is as if, along with the Nag Hammadi Library we had discovered a sect of Valentinians or Sethians that has also survived. Is gnosis transmitted from person to person by tradition, of which apostolic succession is a variety, or does the spirit blow where it will? Perhaps structures, forms, traditions, rituals and dogma are all vehicles in which gnosis can exist for a time and be transmitted to humans, until the rules and pomp overwhelm the inner life and the spirit must look elsewhere for its recipients.

Most of Mandaean history remains mysterious although it is undeniably ancient: the strong baptismal elements in Mandaeanism match well to first- and second-century Jewish and Jewish-Christian baptismal sects. Even the least adventurous of scholars date them to the third century, while many respected experts (including Buckley) think they come from the mid first century.

The Mandaean figure of John the Baptist continues to puzzle modern Western scholars. Luperi asks:

> 'If the Mandaeans are actually the direct descen-
> dants of John's disciples, why do they not have
> any traditions of their own concerning their
> founder but derive everything they have to say
> about him from Christian tradition, sometimes
> even dating from some centuries after the New
> Testament? However, if the Mandaeans have
> always been where they are now and are not
> related directly to John the Baptist, why did they
> go and "recycle" a saint (and only that one!) from
> a rival and hostile religion?'

Well, of course, they may have used the figure of John because he was a *baptizer*, like themselves, and also because in the Gospel of John, John the Baptist is denigrated in order to raise up Jesus. But still, it is at least *possible* that John the Baptist had some connection with the Mandaeans. They do not claim him as their founder, but say instead that he was a prophet.

We know that the Mandaeans had some contact with the Manichaeans because of shared material evidenced in Mandaean and Manichaean texts. Until the discovery and translation of the Cologne Mani Codex, which states that Mani was a member of the Elkasaite sect, some scholars had proposed that Mani had been raised as a Mandaean. Whatever the actuality, there are definite overlaps between Mandaean and Manichaean mythology and contact between the two sects is quite feasible. Indeed, the long life of the Mandaean sect raises the possibility of all sorts of contact with other Gnostic or esoteric groups.

The Mandaeans first emerged into verifiable Western history around the end of the thirteenth century when Ricoldo da Montecroce, a Dominican monk from Tuscany, wrote about his extensive travels in the Middle East. In Baghdad, where he debated against Muslim scholars and was working on a Latin translation of the Qur'an, he was invited to visit 'Sabeans' who dwelled in the nearby desert. These Sabeans were unmistakably Mandaeans. He mentions their language which seems to be halfway between Syriac and Arabic, their reverence for John the Baptist, and their continual water rites.

But it was not until the sixteenth century that the Mandaeans were 'rediscovered' by the Portuguese, who called them St John Christians, incorrectly believing the John of the Mandaeans to be John the Evangelist, not John the Baptist. The Portuguese writers all believed the Mandaeans to be some sort of Christian, perhaps some strange kind of Syrian Christians who had never been converted to the Catholic faith. Perhaps there are further accounts in Arabic writings waiting to be uncovered by Western scholars.

Mandaeans typically worked as silversmiths (an occupation largely forbidden to Muslims), ironsmiths and shipbuilders; they rejected celibacy and did not fast, and Sunday was the Mandaean Sabbath. In 1831 there was a massive interruption in the trans- mission of Mandaean ideas and practices when all of the

Mandaean priests died of cholera and were succeeded by their sons. They do not seem to have believed in reincarnation or in repeating cycles of the world, but they divided history into four sections, like gold, silver, bronze and lead ages. From Adam until the end of the world was 480,000 years. Each successive age was shorter than the last. The first age began with Adam and Eve, but all of humanity, with the exception of one couple, named Ram and Rud, was destroyed by sword and plague. The second age began with Ram and Rud repopulating the world, but humanity again deteriorated until it was destroyed by fire. Another surviving couple, Surbai and Sarhab'il (Lupieri spelling), began the third age, which ended in the flood. The hero of the flood was Sum bar Nu, the equivalent of Shem son of Noah. Like other Semitic peoples (and the name Semitic itself derives from Shem, just as the Hamitic people, for example the Egyptians, are said to derive from Ham) the Mandaeans derive their ancestry from Shem, but they do not acknowledge the validity of the Jews or Arabs as Semites, and the Mandaeans trace other races back to the illegitimate (to them) sons of Noah Ham, Japhet and Iam (an invented character to take the place of Shem who is the Mandaeans' ancestor).

The fourth, and final age, is our current age. The previous epochs were destroyed by sword and plague, by fire, by water, and now the final age will be destroyed 'from the air'. The military planes that have been flying so frequently over Iraq in the past few years must have put the wind up the Mandaeans. And with good reason. Saddam Hussein was no great friend to the Mandaeans, but sometimes his policies against the Kurds resulted in more favourable conditions for the Mandaeans in Iraq. But since the Western coalition has invaded the country, things have gone from bad to worse, and longstanding religious resentments have come to the surface.

Some Mandaeans have been able to flee to the West, and there are small Mandaean communities in the USA in New Jersey and California, in some major cities in Britain and Italy, and particularly in Australia, where the only Mandaean temple, or Mandi, outside of Iraq and Iran has been built. There are Mandaeans also in Odessa and Ukraine, and countries near Iraq like Syria and Jordan have accepted Mandaean refugees.

Before the recent Iraq War, the number of Mandaeans was estimated at something over 100,000 – 75,000 in Iraq and 30,000 in Iran.[89] Now the numbers may be as few as 5,000 in Iraq, with 90 per cent of the Mandaeans of Iraq fleeing their home country. Between 2003 and 2006 in Iraq, there were 106 murders of Mandaeans and 208 kidnaps and they are facing cultural extermination and actual genocide. The Western alliance has not been recognizing the Mandaeans as a significant minority group and as conditions have become more chaotic in Iraq, so their suffering has increased. Some lucky Mandaeans may escape to the West, but the chances of them continuing their religious culture are slight, and Mandaeans who marry non-Mandaeans are effectively producing children who cannot continue their religious traditions.

The Mandaeans and Yezidis (or Yazidis) are both suffering terribly in the Iraq of 2008. Both are ancient, minority sects whose beliefs, and even their mere existence, are largely unknown to the West. The origins of the Yezidis are even more obscure than those of the Mandaeans. Perhaps the Yezidis could be Gnostics too?

The Yezidis are not generally treated as Gnostics, but they

do seem to be dualists, and have other aspects in common with Gnostic groups. They have an ultimate God, and seven angels below him, which suggests a theology that was originally emanationist. The lowest angel was the Peacock god, but he made his way into the darkness, which to some extent coexisted with the light from the beginning. The Peacock Angel created the world, and is the figure that the Yezidis worship. If the Peacock Angel is the demiurge, then the Yezidis have taken the unusual step of worshipping the demiurge instead of the transcendent God.

The Yezidi *Book of Revelation* states that 'I lead to the straight path without a revealed book; I direct aright my beloved and chosen ones by unseen means.' This could perhaps be interpreted as gnosis, a direct path free of doctrine. They have also reinterpreted Genesis, or at least the tradition of Adam and Eve. In their hands, Adam and Eve has become a myth of two races. They consider themselves descendants of Adam, and the true race, whereas all others are descendants of Eve. However, the Yezidis' claim not to have a revealed book (despite the *Book of Revelation* and the *Black Book* being written in the first person) did not recommend them to Muslims, who respected other religions that could be interpreted as being 'People of the Book'.

It would truly be a tragedy if heterodox religious groups like the Mandaeans and Yezidis, who have survived for so long in the Middle East and who have transmitted Gnostic ideas and practices down through the centuries, should face extermination because of Western military intervention, particularly at a time when the West is so open to Gnostic ideas.

CHAPTER 11

REVIVAL

B y the end of the fourteenth century the Cathars were virtually extinguished, and, after a bit of mopping up by the Inquisition, they were finally eradicated in the early fifteenth century. During the latter stages of their persecution they had joined forces with the Waldensians, a Christian sect which was perceived as heretical but which was not Gnostic. The Waldensians, with their ethical and moral concerns, were more akin to the Protestants who would later arrive on the scene, and they have survived in tiny numbers into the twenty-first century.

The Protestant Reformation led to an explosion of new sects and churches, and Christianity has never been the same since Luther nailed his copy of the 95 *Theses* to the door of the Castle Church in Wittenberg on 31 October 1517. The resulting diversity of Western Christianity changed the nature of the game. Western society would no longer be unified under the Catholic Church, and the fragmentation of European Christianity would coincide with and encourage a growing secularization of the West.

Yet almost as soon as the Cathars had died out, Gnosticism

made its way back into Europe in the guise of the Hermetic literature. In 1460, a Greek text of the Corpus Hermeticum arrived in Florence and Cosimo de Medici insisted that the ongoing translation of Plato that he had commissioned should be interrupted in order for it to be translated into Latin. The Hermetica had been previously unknown in medieval Europe, but exerted a great influence on the Renaissance, and later in the fifteenth century the Jewish Kabbalah entered into the Christian tradition.

The third-century Church Father Lactanius had assumed that Hermes Trismegistus was a historical character, and that the Hermetica preceded both Plato and Christianity, which would have made the Hermetica more ancient than any known literature apart from the Torah. Unfortunately, much of the enthusiasm over the Hermetica was bound up with this erroneous scholarship, and the influence of the Hermetica declined once the Swiss Calvinist scholar Audubon showed in the early seventeenth century (1614) that the Hermetica must have been written in the first centuries CE.

Paradoxically, the non-Christian Hermetic literature was easier for Renaissance Christians to accept than Christian Gnostic literature – and the Medicis and their entourage were of course all Catholics. The Gnostics were in dialogue with the Bible and with what became Orthodox Christianity and hence in conflict with it. The anti-Gnostic works of the early Church Fathers ensured that the Gnostics were remembered as heretics, not as an unusual brand of early Christians.

The Hermetica are pagan writings, but European Christian scholars were used to incorporating pagan ideas in their theology and philosophy – Aristotle was a huge influence in the Middle Ages, and there was a revival of Neoplatonism in the Renaissance

– so scholars and philosophers had no difficulty in adopting the world-view of the Hermetica. Once Audubon had shown that the Hermetica were not as old as had been assumed, their influence in the general intellectual culture waned considerably, but the writings continued to have an underground influence in occult circles, in Freemasonry, Rosicrucianism and the Western magical tradition.

If we look for individuals within European culture who might seem to be Gnostic, we find ourselves staring at eccentric figures who lived on the margins of their cultures, such as Paracelsus, Boehme, Swedenborg and Blake, and perhaps a case may be made for Goethe, who made the Faust legend his own. The Faust legend itself includes elements of the Simon Magus legend, especially in the section in which Faust summons Helen back from the dead. Faust's relationship with Helen is central to the second part of Goethe's *Faust* and is a traditional part of the Faust tale, but the ultimate source for it is the story of Simon Magus' consort Helena, the reformed prostitute whom he called 'Ennoia' or 'first thought' and who had been incarnated as Helen of Troy in a previous lifetime.

Goethe was an autocratic poet who was unwilling to settle for anyone else's view of reality. In his autobiographical *Poetry and Truth from My Own Life*, he describes his interest in and sympathy with Christian heresies and how he developed his own personal religion: 'Neoplatonism formed the basis; the hermetical, the mystical, the cabalistic also contributed their share...'[90]

Goethe goes on to describe his view of the creation and development of the universe. At the top was a godhead which had gone on producing itself throughout eternity. From the godhead issued a son, and these two went on to issue a third, which formed a classic Christian trinity. But then these three went on to create a fourth principle, which contained a contradiction in that it shared with the trinity its limitless nature and yet was contained and bounded by that trinity. This fourth entity was Lucifer, 'to whom the power of creation was committed from this time, and from whom all other beings were to proceed.' That is, just as in the Paulician, Bogomil and Cathar cosmologies, Lucifer was the demiurge in Goethe's system. Goethe's Lucifer created angels in his likeness, unlimited but existing in him and, surrounded by the glory of all that he had created, he forgot that he was himself a production of the trinity, and believed that he was self-sufficient and that there was no being higher than him.

One part of these angels returned to the higher world, but the other part of them had to stay with Lucifer, and it is this that constituted the fall of the angels. All that is known as matter was a result of this fall, but this was a dense, material universe with no expansion or further possibilities. The angels reacted to this by expanding the universe within themselves, and thus discovered a domain that could have some independence from the influence of Lucifer, and this is when light and what we usually call the creation appeared. In the course of things, it was still necessary to have some element in this material universe that might strive to return to the higher world of the trinity, and for this reason man was created. As in the Gnostic systems, man has the potential to return to the source and therefore be redeemed. So creation is nothing but 'a falling away and a returning to its source'.

Apart from Goethe's version of the Gnostic myth (and it is

likely that he had read the Church Fathers' versions of the Gnostic systems), his poems contain many references to gnosis: 'And then at once turn your gaze inward: you will find the Centre there within...'[91] and 'What man reveres as God is his own innermost being turned inside out.'[92]

Of the many Romantic poets, William Blake is most qualified to be a true Gnostic. Blake is best known for his lyrics from *Songs of Innocence and Experience*, such as 'The Tyger', 'Little Lamb' or 'The Clod and the Pebble', which are still taught in schools all over the English-speaking world. But it is Blake's less popular 'prophetic' books, which actually comprise the bulk of his literary work, that are the most Gnostic. There are uncanny resemblances between the prophetic poems and the original Gnostic texts. Blake's demiurgic mythical characters such as Urizen or Nobodaddy are ignorant world-creators. The mythology is complex and personal and, like the Gnostic texts, requires a large investment of study time if they are to be properly understood. Even the bizarre names and psychological divisions of humanity resemble the Gnostics.

We can be certain that Blake had never read any actual Gnostic texts because in Blake's time none had been translated into English or even printed in their original languages, although as we shall see below, with the discovery of two codices in the late eighteenth century, Gnosticism was definitely in the air.

The enlightenment historian Edward Gibbon included an extraordinarily complimentary chapter on the Gnostics in his *The History of the Decline and Fall of the Roman Empire*. He was perhaps not altogether sincere when he called the Gnostics 'the most polite, the most learned and the most wealthy of the Christian name', but he flattered them when he wrote:

'The success of the Gnostics was rapid and
extensive. They covered Asia and Egypt,
established themselves in Rome, and sometimes
penetrated into the provinces of the West.
For the most part they arose in the second
century, flourished during the third, and were
suppressed in the fourth or fifth, by the
prevalence of more fashionable controversies,
and by the superior ascendant of the reigning
power.'[93]

Blake moved in the same circles as Gibbon but intensely
disliked his eighteenth-century rationalism, and he wrote the
following in a poem in the Rossetti Manuscript:

'Gibbon arose with a lash of steel,
And Voltaire with a wracking wheel:
The Schools, in clouds of learning roll'd,
Arose with War in iron and gold,'

Blake was familiar with Neoplatonic writings through the translations of Thomas Taylor, whom he knew personally. The
influence of Swedenborg was added to the mix, sometimes as
an authority figure against whom Blake rebelled. Blake may also
have had access to accounts of the Gnostics in Church histories
and early encyclopaedias. It is even possible that he could have
read Church Fathers like Irenaeus in the original, for Blake was
a natural linguist and by his middle years could read Greek
quite easily. And by this time ancient Gnostic texts were
starting to come to light again.

In 1769 James Bruce purchased the Bruce Codex, a Coptic

Gnostic codex that contains the *Books of Jeu*. In 1795 the British Museum purchased the Askew Codex from Dr Anthony Askew. The Askew Codex contains the *Pistis Sophia*, and these two codices (along with the Berlin Gnostic Codex found in the late nineteenth century) were our most important Gnostic texts until the discovery of the Nag Hammadi Library. They were not published or translated until well into the late nineteenth century, but their discovery in the late eighteenth coincides with the time that Blake himself was developing his Gnostic vision. Romanticism itself has been held to have a Gnostic element by certain scholars – witness Keats' comment that this world is not a vale of tears, 'but a vale of soul-making'.

Crabb Robinson, a young friend of Blake who was more or less a disciple wrote:

> 'On my obtaining from him the declaration that the Bible was the work of God, I referred to the commencement of Genesis – "In the beginning God created the Heaven & the Earth." But I gained nothing by this, for I was triumphantly told that this God was not Jehovah, but the Elohim, & the doctrine of the Gnostics repeated with sufficient consistency to silence one so unlearned as myself.'

Blake applied inverse exegesis to Milton,

> 'The reason Milton wrote in fetters when he wrote of Angels & God, and at liberty when of Devils & Hell, is because he was a true Poet, and of the Devil's party without knowing it.'[94]

Blake could be very dualistic sometimes, and the following is altogether a piece with Gnostic dualism: 'Mental Things are alone Real; what is call'd Corporeal, Nobody Knows of its Dwelling Place: it is in Fallacy, & its Existence an Imposture.'[95]

* * *

The advent of theosophy in the second half of the nineteenth century coincided with a great interest in the esoteric side of religion, and Mme Blavatsky's *The Secret Doctrine* made frequent reference to the available Gnostic literature – the heresiologists and the *Books of Jeu* and *Pistis Sophia*. The Berlin Gnostic Codex, which contained the *Apocryphon of John* and the *Gospel of Mary*, was discovered at this time too, and sections of some of the Christian apocrypha, such as the *Hymn of the Pearl* from the *Acts of Thomas*, were understood to be Gnostic. The scholar and theosophist G.R.S. Mead made the greatest contribution to popular study of the Gnostics and his books and translations are still in use today.

It is to this period that the foundation of the modern Gnostic Churches belongs, but the roots of the revival were a little earlier and were connected with Templarism. Modern Gnostic organizations are surprisingly churchy in their activities, language and construction, and many of them borrow from Roman Catholic practice. There are a bewildering variety of societies – the Ecclesia Gnostica, Ecclesia Gnostica Cathoica, Ecclesia Gnostica Mysteriorum, Ecclesia Gnostica Universalis, Eglise Gnostique (Catholica) Apostolique, L'Eglise Gnostique, and more, and some of the Churches may seem to have little that is genuinely Gnostic about them.

The Ecclesia Gnostica Catholica, which in its name is unfortunately similar to many other Gnostic Churches, is reminiscent of the Roman Catholic Church in construction and is the ecclesiastical arm of the Crowleyan Order Templis Orientalis. The O.T.O's Gnostic Mass or Liber XV was written by Aleister Crowley and uses themes from Kabbalah and occultism. It is not an attempt to either reconstruct or imitate genuine ancient Gnostic tradition although it does honour the names of 'Simon Magus, Manes [Mani], Pythagoras, Basilides, Valentinus, Bardesanes and Hippolytus, that transmitted the Light of the Gnosis to us their successors and their heirs'. And the following lines of verse seem genuinely Gnostic:

> 'Thou who art I, beyond all I am,
>
> Who hast no nature and no name,
>
> Who art, when all but thou are gone,
>
> Thou, centre and secret of the Sun,'[96]

The ancient Gnostics were beginning to seep back into the esoteric consciousness as far back as the sixteenth century. In 1531, Cornelius Agrippa's *De occulta philosophia* was published, which referred to the Gnostics in unflattering terms as black magicians who held obscene orgies. During the Enlightenment in the eighteenth century, the Gnostics became associated with the Knights Templar as a Templar revival flourished under the influence of freemasonry. According to Peter Partner, who documented the development of the Templar revival, in the late eighteenth century,

> 'The German Masonic bookseller, Friedrich Nicolai,
> produced an idea that the Templar Masons,
> through the medieval Templars, were the eventual
> heirs of an heretical doctrine which originated with

the early Gnostics. He supported this belief by a
farrago of learned references to the writings of
early fathers of the church on heresy, and by
impressive-looking citations from the Syriac.'[97]

The intellectual grounds upon which this connection between
the Templars and the Gnostics were founded were uncertain in
the extreme, and the resulting structure was very wobbly,
depending on false etymologies and wishful thinking, but it
was also very influential. Most theories of esoteric lineage cannot
stand up to the scrutiny of hard scholarship, but it cannot be
denied that the possibility of a direct line of transmission from
the ancient Gnostics is a seductive one.

The supposed connection between Templars, Gnostics and
hideous orgies continued on into the nineteenth century. Joseph
Hammer, an Austrian Orientalist in service to Britain, identified
the Ophites as the specific Gnostic sect from whom the Templars
had obtained their foul practices, and stated that Baphomet, the
mysterious idol which the Templars had been said to worship,
was none other than Achamoth, the Syriac name for Sophia
used by Valentinians in writings such as the yet undiscovered
Gospel of Philip. According to Hammer, the Holy Grail was
Gnostic too.

A rich stew of Gnostics, Templars, Cathars, Manichaeans and
others continued to inspire secret societies in nineteenth-century
Europe. Gabriel Rosetti, the father of the poet Dante Gabriel
Rosetti, wrote a creative history of alternative Christianity in
Europe, in which the Cathars and Templars took pride of place,
in league with Dante, the poet of the *Divine Comedy*, not the
author's son.

What we may now call the established modern Gnostic Churches trace themselves back to the 'Gnostic revival' of 1890s' France. The Gnostic Revival arose out of several streams of interest and was part of the general ferment of occultism and theosophy. France was of course the country of the Cathars, and in 1872–4, Napoleon Peyrat published *Histoire d'Albigenses*, a romanticized vision of the Cathars.

The Universal Catholic Gnostic Church was spiritually founded (without any initial claim to apostolic succession) on 21 September 1890 by Jules Doinel (1842–1902). Doinel was a freemason, a library archivist and a spiritist. His Freemasonry and his growing interest in the Cathars and Gnostics allowed him entry into French esoteric and occult circles, and thus his life overlapped with that of Abbé Saunière, Rennes-le-Château, the Dossiers Secrets and the whole mysterious world of the Prieuré de Sion made famous by *The Holy Blood and the Holy Grail* and *The Da Vinci Code*.

In 1888 Doinel discovered in the library of Orléans a charter dated 1022 which was written by a forerunner of the Cathars, a certain Canon Stephan de Orléans, a cleric who taught dualistic doctrine. This was a genuine historical document connected to an outbreak of heresy by 'Manichaeans' in Orléans.[98] Doinel became fascinated by the Cathars and their predecessors, the Bogomils, Paulicians, Manichaeans, and various other Gnostic movements. As a practising Spiritist he had recurring visions of a divine feminine aspect and he became convinced that it was his destiny to take part in the restoration of the worship of the divine feminine, to give it its proper place in religion, and to reestablish the fallen church of the Sophia.

One night in 1888 Doinel had a vision in which the aeon

Jesus appeared and consecrated him as a patriarch. In the vision, Jesus was assisted by two Bogomil bishops (historically verifiable), and Doinel received instructions to establish a new Church. He attempted to contact other Cathar and Gnostic spirits in seances which were held in the salon of Lady Marie Caithness, the Duchess of Pomar, who was of Spanish origin but married the English Lord Caithness. She considered herself to be the reincarnation of Mary Stuart and was approached around 1882 by H.P. Blavatsky, Colonel Olcott and Annie Besant, to establish the French branch of the Theosophical Society.

In September 1889 Doinel spiritually contacted the 'Very High Synod of Bishops of the Paraclete', which consisted of 41 Cathar bishops whose names were later checked against records from the Bibliothèque Nationale and were proven to be accurate. Doinel began to consecrate a number of bishops and Sophias, a new position in his Church hierarchy that was open to women. Among the first to be consecrated was the famous occultist Papus (Gérard Encausse, 1865–1916), as Tau Vincent. Doinel himself was the Bishop of Montségur (the location of the massacre of the Cathars) and Alet and took the title Tau Valentinus II, considering himself a successor to Valentinus. The title 'Tau' (the letter Tau resembles a truncated cross and already had a history of occult exegesis) has continued to be used by Gnostic bishops, namely Tau Stephanus (Stephan Hoeller) and the author Tau Malachi.

The theology of Doinel's Gnostic Church was a mixture of the doctrine of Simon Magus, Valentinus and the Marcus, all of which could only be known from the writings of the Church Fathers, even though *Pistis Sophia* was ascribed to Valentinus by the Church.

Suddenly, however, in 1895, Doinel converted back to Roman Catholicism and became an apostate to his own Church. He wrote articles in which he denounced the organizations that were once so dear to him, publishing in 1895 his denunciation of Freemasonry in his book *Lucifer Démasqué* (Lucifer Unmasked) using the pseudonym Jean Kostka. Yet he also later wrote for René Guénon's *Gnosis* and co-authored a Gnostic catechism with Guénon. In 1900 Doinel requested readmission as a bishop in the Gnostic Church, and he was reconsecrated by Synésius as Tau Jules, Bishop of Alet and Mirepoix. He died in 1902, after a turbulent religious and spiritual life, perhaps having become apostate once again.

* * *

It is difficult to admit an uninterrupted line of historical Gnostic descent from the Sethians, Valentinians, Hermetists, Manichaeans, Bogomils or Cathars to any modern Gnostic Church, but Churches like Stephan Hoeller's Ecclesia Gnostica certainly pay attention to the new discoveries of Gnostic scriptures. The members of these particular Gnostic Churches have taken to heart the truism that Gnosticism is a way of knowledge, and many leading members are exceedingly well informed about their spiritual inheritance, know their texts inside out and keep up with the extensive scholarship that surrounds Gnosticism and the Nag Hammadi Library.

Many modern Gnostic Churches claim apostolic succession via the Roman Catholic Church. Apostolic succession might seem to be unnecessary for Gnostics, and in many Gnostic texts – such as the *Gospel of Philip*, which sometimes criticizes the 'apostolic men', or the *Gospel of Judas*, in which the disciples are shown to be worshippers of the demiurge – apostolic succession would

appear to be a distinct disadvantage. But many of the members
of the modern Gnostic Churches were brought up Catholic, and
feel, as ultimately do the members of Protestant Churches, that
a direct line of descent from Christ's disciples is important.

Perhaps we should also remember that Simon Magus,
Basilides and Valentinus were all alleged to have been taught by
apostles or the disciples of apostles. The modern Gnostic claims
to apostolic succession rely on a quirk of priestly ordination,
according to which the section of Hebrews (5:4–6) which refers
to 'a priest forever unto the order of Melchizedek', is interpreted as meaning that, once ordained, a priest or bishop can
never have his status removed, even if expelled from the Church,
and a bishop would then be able to consecrate and ordain other
bishops and priests.

Joseph René Vilatte, a Wisconsin Old Catholic received con-
secration as bishop from the Syrian Jacobite Church in Ceylon
in 1892 and subsequently consecrated several other bishops,
including Gnostic bishops, in North America and France. The
Roman Catholic Church apparently disputes this interpretation
as 'valid yet illicit', but there are now lineages of independent
priests and bishops who have taken advantage of this loophole.[99]

Sacramental practices, the Eucharist in particular, are
important to the new Gnostic Churches, who reason that since
the Eucharist, baptism and other rites were important to the
ancient Gnostics they should therefore have a place in any
revival. An English-based Gnostic Church, the Pre-Nicene
Gnostic Catholic Church, was founded by Richard Duc de
Palatine (Richard Powell, 1916–78), an Australian of French
descent. Duc de Palatine was initially ordained in the Liberal
Catholic Church and, in 1953, was consecrated a bishop by an

independent bishop, Mar Georgius I (Hugh George de Willmott Newman), Patriarch of Glastonbury. Duc de Palatine consecrated Stephan Hoeller in 1967 and Hoeller went on to found his own Los Angeles-based Ecclesia Gnostica. Hoeller was to become a considerable scholar and a prodigious lecturer in the fields of the Western occult and esoteric tradition and Gnosticism, and his Gnostic Church has accommodated the various twentieth-century textual discoveries.

Also prominent is the Apostolic Johannite Church, which owes its origins to the French neo-Templar movement in the early nineteenth century, but in its form is more connected to Doinel's Gnostic restoration. Its founder, Bernard Raymond Fabré-Palaprat, found a version of the Gospel of John in Greek, titled the *Evangelikon* (apparently on a second-hand bookstall – it was quite possible to find rare and unique ancient manuscripts at that time, witness the Bruce and Askew codices), which contained none of the miracles, and also presented Christ as an initiate of Osiris. Along with this version of John's gospel was the *Levitikon*, a description of the Knights Templars and their esoteric organization. Neither the *Evangelikon* nor the *Levitikon* could be as ancient as Fabré-Palaprat assumed, and the lack of miracles in the *Evangelikon* seems more like a characteristic of the rationalist enlightenment, in keeping with Thomas Jefferson's attempt at a critical New Testament from which miracles and the supernatural were banished.

* * *

Gnosticism resurfaced in many forms in the twentieth century. Jung made explicit use of Gnostic ideas in his writings. He himself had strange experiences and wrote his inspired mystical work *Seven Sermons to the Dead* in the name of Basilides. Jung was the lucky recipient of the Jung Codex, Codex I of the Nag Hammadi Library. The Gnostics were claimed as existentialist by the influential scholar of Gnosticism, Hans Jonas, but the twentieth-century existentialists did not return the favour and designate themselves Gnostic. Although many attitudes towards experience and awareness might be shared by Gnostics and existentialists, the presence of a higher world (of which our world is a fallen shadow), which is truer and more real than our material reality, is essential to Gnosticism and incompatible with existentialism.

G.I. Gurdjieff was an Armenian of Greek extraction who brought his teaching to Europe and North America. His most famous interpreter was P.D. Ouspensky, a Russian esotericist and seeker who had been sifting through religious, theosophical and occult literature for hidden knowledge and searching for spiritual schools that could offer a practical approach to awakening that would be suitable for Westerners. Having travelled to India, Ouspensky found what he was looking for back in St Petersburg in the figure of Gurdjieff.

Neither Gurdjieff nor his pupils claimed to be Gnostics, and Gurdjieff could have had little direct knowledge of the Gnostics. The Theosophist G.R.S. Mead, who founded the Quest Society and was later a personal friend of Ouspensky, published many books on the available sources, but Gurdjieff showed little sign of being interested in scholarship beyond his formative years, so Gurdjieff's actual knowledge of Gnosticism must have been slight. Despite having lived in France for more than 25 years, Gurdjieff is, to my knowledge, not on record as having referred to the Cathars either, although he did make extravagant claims concerning the Essenes – that he had brought music from the

Essene monastery where Jesus Christ had studied, for instance (there was plenty of interest in the Essenes prior to the Dead Sea Scrolls discovery, based on the sketchy accounts in the works of such ancient writers as Philo and Pliny). But Gurdjieff had travelled extensively, laboured hard and had studied in various esoteric schools.

It is possible that Gurdjieff may have been exposed to Gnostic currents. His home country, Armenia, was a crossroads of culture, containing diverse elements of East and West. As we have seen, many Gnostic or related groups had connections with Armenia. Valentinians were seemingly in the area in the late seventh century, and there were Paulicians in Armenia. Edessa, an ancient centre of Syrian Christian activity connected with the name of St Thomas, and a possible locale for the compilation of the *Gospel of Thomas*, was formerly part of Armenia. There may have been Mandaeans in the area, and there were certainly Yezidis. Gurdjieff himself saw a Yezidi boy trapped inside a chalk circle and was very curious about their culture.

In any case, Gurdjieff's ideas, which come from many esoteric sources, and his own genius, have many Gnostic features. Gurdjieff taught that we are asleep, but that we can wake up, and this concept (which is more than a metaphor) is central to Gurdjieff's teaching. The Gnostics would certainly have agreed with him:

> 'This is the way each one has acted, as though
> asleep at the time when he was ignorant. And this
> is the way he has come to gnosis, as if he had
> awakened. It is good for the man who will return
> and awaken.'[100]

Like the Gnostics, Gurdjieff used myth as the vehicle for the permanent legacy of his teaching in his writings *Beelzebub's Tales to his Grandson* and *Meetings with Remarkable Men*. In *Beelzebub's Tales* there is something wrong with the world. A cosmic catastrophe was unforeseen by the forces above and as a result the higher powers had to insert an organ, kundabuffer, into the spines of human beings, which made them see reality incorrectly. The organ was removed eventually, but the effects of kundabuffer had crystallized in human beings, and so they continued to be ignorant of their true situations in the universe. Sacred individuals were then sent to awaken mankind and free them from the consequences of the kundabuffer. *Beelzebub's Tales* employs inversionary devices, such as making Beelzebub, traditionally a devil, the hero of the story, or making Western civilization, the legacy of the Greeks and the Romans, the cause of many of the problems of the contemporary world.

Gurdjieff's Ray of Creation is an emanationist theology, which begins with an Absolute, from whom worlds are produced from higher worlds but, at least in his initial expression, this is expressed using the terms of nineteenth- or twentieth-century science, with the levels of creation having physical representation in the galaxies, suns and planets. As with the Manichaeans, the souls go to the moon upon death, though with somewhat different implications. Gurdjieff even once said that: 'The way of the development of hidden possibilities is against nature, against God.'[101] It is surely not the Absolute, Gurdjieff's equivalent of the ultimate God, that is intended there.

Anthony Blake, a leading interpreter of Gurdjieff, called his teachings,

> 'Gnosticism without the trappings, couched in a
> language which every educated Western man
> has the possibility of understanding... There is a
> whole structure of teaching on this planet. It is
> like a strange other-dimensional house in which
> the rooms can act like "keys" to other doors.
> Gurdjieff is a key to unlock the doors to certain
> rooms called "Sufism", "Gnosticism", and so on.
> These in their turn are keys to unlock the door
> marked "Gurdjieff".'[102]

Gurdjieff's disturbing parable of the shepherd is Gnostic to the core. Gurdjieff's shepherd is a rich but stingy magician who did not want to hire men to look after his sheep. The sheep ran away because they knew that the magician wanted their flesh, and they wandered off or died. He found a solution:

> 'He hypnotized his sheep and suggested to
> them, first of all, that they were immortal and
> that no harm was being done to them when they
> were skinned; that on the contrary, it would be
> very good for them and even pleasant... Further,
> the magician suggested to his sheep that they
> were not sheep at all; to some of them he
> suggested that they were lions, to some that they
> were eagles, to some that they were men, to
> others that they were magicians.'[103]

Who could this magician be but the Gnostic demiurge?

* * *

The Nag Hammadi Library was discovered in 1945, but was only published in full in the 1970s. Since the 1970s, Gnostic ideas have begun to permeate the more interesting pockets of pop culture, and, who knows, the Nag Hammadi texts may prove to be as influential in our era as the rediscovered *Corpus Hermeticum* was in the Renaissance.

In terms of modern thinkers, the science fiction author Philip K. Dick is often claimed as a modern Gnostic. He had strange psychological experiences, visions of the early Christian centuries, intimations of a God-equivalent named 'VALIS' (Vast Active Living Intelligence System), and saw a beam of pink light that gave him access to perceptions and intelligence that he otherwise would not have experienced. Dick investigated Gnostic literature and there are strong Gnostic themes in his novels.

So too for the comics of graphic novel writer Alan Moore. There are Gnostic themes in his earlier works, such as the revelation that the entire history of the generic superhero Marvelman was actually artificial memories implanted in him by his creator, and is thus a dream from which he awakens. In *V For Vendetta*, released as a film in 2006 without Moore's approval, the grim totalitarian Britain of Moore's story is a backdrop against which Evey's degradation and transformation can occur. At the age of 40, Moore proclaimed himself as a magician, and an occult-oriented Gnosticism has been at the core of his life and work ever since.

In the 1990s virtual reality became a popular theme and the concept lent itself to a Gnostic interpretation. Movies like *The Truman Show* and particularly *The Matrix* used the relationship between electronic media and 'real life' as an analogy between our ordinary lives and the spiritual life. But these movies could only take the Gnostic vision so far. The derelict, embattled city of Zion in *The Matrix* is hardly the Gnostic Pleroma and *The Matrix* sequels (literally) lost the plot and moved away from the genuinely Gnostic themes of the original movie.

Philip Pullman's *His Dark Materials* trilogy was influenced by Pullman's reading of the Gnostics and Blake. In the books, Pullman's universe may be considered dualistic in that there is matter and dust, a quality that is akin to consciousness. The Church worships the Authority, is opposed to free thought and attempts to suppress knowledge about dust. In the final book, the Authority, a shrivelled, pitiful thing, dies and it is revealed that he lied about his importance. He was not the creator of the universe, merely the first conscious being to appear. It is dust that is fundamental to being, not any anthropomorphic God figure. Pullman admires the Gnostics, Blake and Milton in particular (a case may be made for Milton being a Gnostic, with his placing of Satan as a figure of fundamental importance in the universe and his occasional passages of spiritual grandeur), but he is not a Gnostic himself. He is an atheist, something that has bothered both orthodox Christians (particularly the Roman Catholics who see his portrayal of the Church of the Authority as a direct dig at theirs) and those readers who have seen Gnostic and spiritual value in *His Dark Materials*. In the third book, Pullman is unequivocal about Christianity, 'The Christian religion is a very powerful and convincing mistake, that's all.'[104]

Myths can be spontaneously generated in response to spiritual and cultural needs, drawing on whatever material is available, even in the twentieth and twenty-first centuries. At the end of the twentieth century, we have evidence of a fascinating spontaneous flowering of a Gnostic viewpoint. In a 1997 article in the *Miami New Times*[105] journalist Lynda Edwards looked at the myths produced by homeless children in Miami. Though this was a heart-rending account, she focused not so much on their plight as on the communal myths that the younger children had created. The myths have a definite dualistic, Gnostic quality to them, put into a modern context, and the article had a considerable influence. At one point the story was going to be adapted into a film, *Bloody Mary*, with a script by horror writer Clive Barker. The article described the folklore that had developed among the homeless children, who were used to chaotic, violent lives, moving from one homeless shelter to another, until they were forced back out onto the streets by their homeless parents.

The children's lives were full of violence – gang violence, violence from their own parents or from other homeless people – drug abuse, sexual abuse, gun crime, burglary. They received little in the way of explanation for their situations and had little hope of improvement in their lives, little in the way of meaningful role models from their parents. The mythology that they developed is a mish-mash of folkloric figure, gods from the Santeria or Yoruba religion, characters from popular movies and hints of a form of Christianity that has been turned on its head.

As with Gnosticism, their myths are syncretistic, combining elements from different traditions, and are also dualistic. In their stories, angels and demons war overhead for the fate of the city and the homeless children. The blue lady, a kind but elusive angel apparently derived from Santeria, has an evil counterpart, Bloody Mary or La Llorona, who weeps black tears. Bloody Mary is a worldwide folkloric figure who is invoked by children in a game involving mirrors and chanting. Some of the homeless children have decided that the malignant Bloody Mary was once Mary the mother of Jesus, a piece of startling inverse exegesis.

Like the Gnostic archons, 'the demons are nourished by dark human emotions: jealousy, hate, fear.' Satan has a direct influence over the city, but God has fled, and is often seen as a doctor who is so busy that he is usually inaccessible. Thus the distinction between a lower God who directly controls the world with his archons and a true God who is alienated from the world has spontaneously emerged in the myths of these homeless children.

But what their myth system might lack is any central notion of real gnosis. There are bad states of mind that feed the demons, and children can be possessed by demons, but the only way for the children to really help themselves is by praying to the blue lady. Still, the metaphysical knowledge of their true situation is highly prized by the children. One boy stated suggestively, 'And when I do good, it makes their fighting easier – I know it! I *know*!'

* * *

What are the advantages of a Gnostic viewpoint? Why would anyone in the modern age want to follow teachings and systems that ceased to be living religions between 600 and 1,600 years ago? Should a modern Gnostic take the rituals and the myths literally? The Manichaeans obviously did – they really thought that they were liberating Light when they ate their figs and melons. Should we really think that an ignorant demiurge rules this world, a lion-headed inferior God with blazing eyes? Are archons regulating the world, perhaps resembling the aliens of

David Icke's mythology? Of course not. That way lies paranoia. Modern Gnostics can no more take seriously the Gnostic myths as literal truth than Valentinian Gnostics interpreted the New Testament literally. The Gnostic systems can be 'a myth to live by', as Joseph Campbell wrote. The Gnostics were flexible in their mythology, always reinterpreting, inverting, refining, expanding their central myths. It is this contradictory, capricious, unpredictable element that so confounds scholars when they try to define Gnosticism.

We all have some pretty base motives in our lives that are to do with satisfying our needs – physical, emotional, social, maintaining our weaknesses, seeking pleasure, avoiding pain or discomfort. But in our highest moments we glimpse a world that is different to this. According to the Gnostics, this world is more real than the world of the body and matter, or even more real than the inner world of everyday emotions, sensation and the chain of associations that constitutes our inner lives. The world of the spirit, or the Pleroma, or the realm of the true God or good God, is more real than the world of matter, and it precedes that world. Although absolute dualists such as the Manichaeans view the principles of light and darkness as eternally coexisting, our world, in which the two are combined, was a subsequent creation.

The Gnostic view of the world may initially seem bleak or even negative, but it offers hope. This world is denigrated in most Gnostic systems, it is true, as inferior to the experience of the Pleroma. The dark matter that houses the world is inferior to the seeds of light contained within us. The bride prefers the spiritual bridegroom to the thieves and adulterers. The spiritual Eve offers Adam a truth that the archons cannot give him. The saviour rescues Sophia and returns her to the Pleroma. The particles of light are freed and return to the King of Light, and we, who are the light, return also.

Perhaps what we need is another Gnostic saviour figure. Or perhaps not. If the Pleroma sent a saviour figure today, he would probably end up seduced by the many goodies that the archons could offer him. If the prince in the *Hymn of the Pearl* forgot his mission merely because of the food of Egypt, how might a modern Gnostic saviour cope with flocks of adoring disciples, fleets of Rolls Royces, an endless supply of fresh girls (or boys)? Perhaps a female saviour figure, an incarnation of Sophia, would be less susceptible to the lures of the archons, or might have more experience in falling and rising again. Or perhaps the Gnostics were onto something when they looked back to mythical figures like Seth, Enoch, Manda dHayye or Jesus (who may as well have been mythical to them).

During the course of historical Gnosticism there were many meetings and remeetings of the different Gnostic groups. Sethians attached and detached themselves from Christianity and Platonism, Valentinians perhaps adapted Sethian ideas, Mandaeans probably encountered Sethians and Manichaeans, who in turn influenced Paulicians and Bogomils, who in turn influenced Cathars. But we are the first people to encounter the writings of all these different groups. Perhaps we have a responsibility to the ancient and medieval Gnostics who have bequeathed their world-views to us? Certainly the opportunities for Gnosis are greater now than they may have been for several centuries.

REFERENCES

1 For example, Barnstone and Meyer's *The Gnostic Bible* (Boston, 2003).

2 Trans. Layton.

3 John Turner, 'Sethian Gnosticism: A Literary History', in *Nag Hammadi Gnosticism and Early Christianity* (Peabody, 1986).

4 See Carl Smith, *No Longer Jews* (Peabody, 2004), p. 224.

5 Giovanni Filoramo, *A History of Gnosticism* (Oxford, 1990), p. 173.

6 *Ante-Nicene Fathers*, vol. 1, p. 352.

7 *Zostrianos*, in *The Nag Hammadi Library in English*.

8 Benjamin Walker, *Gnosticism: Its History and Influence* (Wellingborough, 1983), p. 57.

9 For a translation and full commentary on both the *Exegesis on the Soul* and the *Hymn of the Pearl*, see my book *Gnostic Writings on the Soul: Annotated & Explained*.

10 Robinson, *The Nag Hammadi Library in English*, p. 306.

11 Karen L. King, *What is Gnosticism?* (London, 2003), p. 210.

12 Quoted in Merkur, *Gnosis*, p. 126.

13 Rudolph, *Gnosis*, p. 173.

14 *Ante-Nicene Fathers*, vol. 1, Irenaeus I.XXI.5.

15 Rudolph, *Gnosis*, p. 70.

16 The book entitled *The Gnostic Bible* by Barnstone and Meyer is a modern compilation of Gnostic texts from all periods of Gnosticism.

17 http://www.hypotyposeis.org/papers/theodotus.htm, trans. Robert Pierce Casey.

18 *Ante-Nicene Fathers*, vol. 1, p. 317.

19 See David Fideler, *Jesus Christ, Son of God: Ancient Cosmology and Early Christian Symbolism* (Whaton, 1993).

20 Elaine Pagels, *The Gnostic Paul*, p. 5.

21 Layton, *The Gnostic Scriptures*, p. 439.

22 Quotations from the *Gospel of Thomas* are from my own translation.

23 William Arnal and others.

24 April DeConick.

25 *The Gospel of Philip Annotated & Explained* (Skylight Paths Publishing, 2006).

26 Epistle to the Trallians 9:1f, quoted in Earl Doherty, *The Jesus Puzzle* (Ottawa, 2005) p. 305.

27 Excerpts from *Theodotus* 26 (http://www.hypotyposeis.org/papers/theodotus.htm).

28 I would not advise the reader to try out ascetic practices such as fasting or sleep deprivation without professional advice or a strong faculty of self-criticism.

29 'The Interpretation of Knowledge', from *The Nag Hammadi Library in English* (HarperCollins, 2000).

30 See his *Rethinking Gnosticism* (Princeton, 1999).

31 Epiphanius, Panarion (http://essenes.crosswinds.net/panarion.html).

32 en.wikipedia.org/wiki/Jamais-vu.

33 Plotinus, *Enneads* II 9, 14, quoted in Rudolph, *Gnosis*, p. 223.

34 Origen, *Contra Celsum*, book VI, in the *Ante-Nicene Fathers*.

35 Contra Celsum, book VI. XXXVIII, in the *Ante-Nicene Fathers*, vol. IV.

36 See John Turner, *To See the Light: A Gnostic Appropriation of Jewish Priestly Practice and Sapiential and Apocalyptic Visionary Lore* (The University of Nebraska-Lincoln).

37 John D. Turner, 'Ritual in Gnosticism,' in *Society of Biblical Literature Seminar Papers* (Atlanta, 1994), pp. 136–81 (http://jdt.unl.edu/ritual.htm).

38 Irenaeus 1. XXI.3 in the The Ante-Nicene Fathers Vol. 1.

39 *Catechism of the Catholic Church* (Our Sunday Visitor, 2000), p. 249.

40 Irenaeus I.XXI 3, in *The Ante-Nicene Fathers*.

41 Ibid, XXI.2.

42 Ibid, I.XXI.4.

43 See Marvin Meyer, *Ancient Christian Magic: Coptic Texts of Ritual Power* (San Francisco, 1994).

44 Violet MacDermot, *The Fall of Sophia: A Gnostic Text on the Redemption of Universal Consciousness* (Great Barrington, 2001), pp. 115–16.

45 *Excerpts from Theodotus*, p. 78 (http://www.hypotyposeis.org/papers/theodotus.htm).

46 At the time of writing, in 2008, the Samaritans survive by the skin of their teeth, and by their own count their population is numbered at a tiny 705. The twenty-first century is seeing the imminent disappearance of many ancient minority religious groups, as we shall see in Chapter 10 with the Mandaeans.

47 Theodore Vrettos, *Alexandria: City of the Western Mind* (New York, 2001), p. 3.

48 Clement Salaman et al, *The Way of Hermes* (Rochester, VT, 2000), p. 10.

49 Ibid, p. 40.

50 Hans Jonas, *The Gnostic Religion* (Boston, 1963), p. 206.

51 Rudolph, *Gnosis*, p. 335.

52 Jonas, *The Gnostic Religion*, p. 215.

53 Ibid, p. 213.

54 Many elements of Gnostic cosmogony have been combined and reconfigured by Mani or his successors, particularly the notion of the anthropos, the divine archetypal idea of the human.

55 Ibid, p. 218.

56 Indian traditions, Neoplatonism and G.I. Gurdjieff have also claimed that the soul goes to the moon, though each views this in a somewhat different way.

57 Rudolph, *Gnosis*, p. 290.

58 See http://www.pr.mq.edu.au/macnews/
ShowItem.asp?ItemID=419.

59 For accessible histories of Gnosticism that take in most of the
Western esoteric tradition, see Richard Smoley's *Forbidden
Faiths* (New York, 2006) and Tobias Churton's *Gnostic
Philosophy* (Rochester, 2005).

60 Merkur, *Gnosis*, p. 189.

61 *Plotinus: The Enneads*, trans. John Dillon (Harmondsworth,
1991), p. 422.

62 See 'Advaita and Gnosticism', in the Research Bulletin of the
Vishveshvarananda Vedic Research Institute (Hoshiarupur,
India), 2003.

63 See Carl Ernst, 'Fragmentary Versions of the Apocryphal
"Hymn of the Pearl" in Arabic, Turkish, Persian and Urdu', in
Jerusalem Studies in Arabic and Islam, vol. 31 (Jerusalem,
2006). See also http://www.unc.edu/~cernst/
articles/2006c.doc.

64 Merkur, *Gnosis*, p. 201.

65 Meyer/Barnstone, *The Gnostic Bible* (Shambhala, 2003),
p. 664.

66 Our single account of Paulician doctrine is in the surviving
works of the Byzantine writer Peter of Sicily, in his Sermons
and the *Useful History, Refutation and Overthrowing of the Void
and Idle Heresy of the Manichaeans a.k.a Paulicians.*

67 Stephen O'Shea, *The Perfect Heresy: The Revolutionary Life and
Death of the Medieval Cathars* (New York, 2000), p. 23.

68 Couliano, *The Tree of Gnosis*, p. 208.

69 Sean Martin, *The Cathars* (Harpenden, 2006), pp. 50–1.

70 Stephen O'Shea, *The Perfect Heresy: The Revolutionary Life and
Death of the Medieval Cathars*, p.13.

71 Ioan Couliano, *The Tree of Gnosis* (San Francisco, 1992), p. 231.

72 Ibid, p. 222.

73 Ibid, p. 218.

74 O'Shea, *The Perfect Heresy*, p. 41.

75 Ibid, pp. 275–6.

76 Ibid, p. 44.

77 Ibid, p. 23.

78 See Couliano, *The Tree of Gnosis*, p. 223.

79 Aubrey Burl, *God's Heretics: The Albigensian Crusade* (Sutton, 2006), pp. xv–vii.

80 O'Shea, pp. 30–1.

81 Ibid, p. 6.

82 Ibid. p. 5.

83 http://en.wikipedia.org/wiki/Châteaux_de_Lastours.

84 Jacques Lacarrière (San Francisco, 1989), p. 7.

85 Edmondo Lupieri, *The Mandaeans: The Last Gnostics* (Grand Rapids, 2002), p. 44.

86 Rudolph, *Gnosis,* p. 359.

87 Translated into English by G.R.S. Mead as *Gnostic John the Baptizer: Selections from the Mandæan John-Book*, available in many reprint editions, e.g. the facsimile edition by Kessinger Publishing, 1993.

88 Lupieri, *The Mandaeans*, p. 43.

89 Barnstone and Meyer, *The Gnostic Bible*, p. 535.

90 Johann von Goethe, *Poetry and Truth From My Own Life* (London, 1908), Book VIII, p. 313.

91 Johann von Goethe, *Selected Verse*, Harmondsworth, 1982, p. 276.

92 Ibid, p. 278.

93 Edward Gibbon, *The History of the Decline and Fall of the Roman Empire*, Chapter XV.

94 'The Marriage of Heaven and Hell'.

95 *A Vision of the Last Judgement*.

96 Aleister Crowley, The Gnostic Mass (www.sacred-texts.com/oto/lib15.htm).

97 Peter Partner, *The Knights Templar and Their Myth* (Rochester, 1990), p. 129.

98 See Walter L. Wakefield, *Heresies of the High Middle Ages* (New York, 1991), pp. 74-81.

99 For apostolic succession, see Jay Kinney's article, 'Gnosticism: Ancient and Modern' (http://www.gnostic.info/kinney_gnosticism.html).

100 *Gospel of Truth*, author's translation.

101 P.D. Ouspensky, *In Search of the Miraculous* (London, 1950), p. 47.

102 Anthony Blake, *An Index to In Search of the Miraculous* (Coombe Springs Press, 1982), pp. iii, vii.

103 *In Search of the Miraculous*, p. 219.

104 Philip Pullman, *The Amber Spyglass*, (London, 2001), p. 464.

105 Lynda Edwards, 'Myths Over Miami' (http://www.miaminew-times.com/1997-06-05/news/myths-over-miami/).

BIBLIOGRAPHY

Angus, S., *The Mystery Religions*. New York: Dover Publications, 1975

Baigent, Michael, Richard Leigh and Henry Lincoln, *The Holy Blood and the Holy Grail*. New York: Doubleday, 2003

Barnstone, Willis, and Martin Meyer, *The Gnostic Bible*. Boston: Shambhala, 2003

BeDuhn, Jason David, *The Manichaean Body: In Discipline and Ritual*. Baltimore: The Johns Hopkins University Press, 2002

Blake, Anthony, *An Index to In Search of the Miraculous*. Coombe Springs Press, 1982

Blake, William, *The Complete Poetry and Prose of William Blake*. Berkeley: University of California Press, 1982

Bloom, Harold, *The Flight to Lucifer*. New York: Vintage Books, 1980

Brown, Dan, *The DaVinci Code*. New York: Doubleday, 2003

Buckley, Jorunn Jacobsen, *The Mandaeans: Ancient Texts and Modern People*. New York: Oxford University Press, 2002

Burl, Aubrey, *God's Heretics: The Albigensian Crusade*. Sutton Publishing, 2006

Cameron, Ron (ed.), *The Other Gospels: Non-Canonical Gospel Texts*. Philadelphia, PA: The Westminster Press, 1982

Churton, Tobias, *The Gnostics*. London: George Weidenfeld & Nicholson, 1987

Gnostic Philosophy: From Ancient Persia to Modern Times. Rochester, VT: Inner Traditions, 2005

Couliano, Ioan P., *The Tree of Gnosis*. HarperSanFrancisco, 1992

Davies, Stevan L., *The Gospel of Thomas and Christian Wisdom*. Oregon House, CA: Bardic Press, 2005

The Gospel of Thomas: Annotated & Explained. Woodstock, VT: Skylight Paths, 2002

The Secret Book of John: Annotated & Explained. Woodstock, VT: Skylight Paths, 2005

De Conick, April, 'The Great Mystery of Marriage: Sex and Conception in Ancient Valentinian Traditions', in *Vigiliae Christianae*, vol. 57, no. 3, July 2003, pp. 307–42. Leiden: Brill, 2003

The Thirteenth Apostle: What the Gospel of Judas Really Says. New York: Continuum, 2007

Doherty, Earl, *The Jesus Puzzle*. Ottawa: Age of Reason Publications, 2005

Doresse, Jean, *The Secret Books of the Egyptian Gnostics*. New York: MJF Books, 1986

Drury, Nevill, *The Dictionary of the Esoteric*. London: Watkins Publishing, 2004

Ehrman, Bart, *Lost Christianities: The Battles for Scripture and the Faiths We Never Knew*. New York: Oxford University Press, 2003

Lost Scriptures: Books That Did Not Make It Into the New Testament. New York: Oxford University Press, 2003

Eliade, Mircea, and Ioan P. Couliano, *The HarperCollins Concise Guide to World Religions*. HarperSanFrancisco, 2000

Elliott, J.K., *The Apocryphal New Testament*. Oxford: Clarendon Press, 1993

Ferreira, Johan, *The Hymn of the Pearl: The Syriac and Greek Texts*, Early Christian Studies 3. Sydney: St Pauls, 2002

Fideler, David, *Jesus Christ, Sun of God: Ancient Cosmology and Early Christian Symbolism*. Wheaton, IL: Quest Books, 1993

Filoramo, Giovanni. *A History of Gnosticism*. Oxford: Blackwell, 1990

Flew, Antony, *A Dictionary of Philosophy*. New York: St Martin's Press, rev. 2nd edn. 1984

Foerster, Werner, trans. R. McL. Wilson, *Gnosis*; vol. 1: *Patristic Evidence*. Oxford: Clarendon, 1972

Fowden, Gareth, *The Egyptian Hermes: A Historical Approach to the Late Pagan Mind*. Princeton University Press, 1993

Freke, Timothy, and Peter Gandy, *Jesus and the Lost Goddess*. New York: Harmony Books, 2000

The Jesus Mysteries. New York: Harmony Books, 1999

Frend, W.H.C., *The Rise of Christianity*. Philadelphia, PA: Fortress Press, 1984

Goethe, Johann W. von, trans. Minna Steele Smith, *Poetry and Truth From My Own Life*. London: George Bell & Sons, 1908

Selected Verse. Harmondsworth: Penguin, 1982

Grant, Robert M., *Gnosticism*. New York: Harper & Brothers, 1961

Gnosticism and Early Christianity. New York: Harper Torchbooks, 1966

Guirdham, Arthur, *The Cathars and Reincarnation*. London: C.W. Daniel, 1990

Gurdjieff, G.I., *Beelzebub's Tales to his Grandson*. New York: Penguin, 1999

Meetings with Remarkable Men. New York: Penguin, 1991

Hoeller, Stephan A., *Gnosticism: New Light on the Ancient Tradition of Inner Knowing*. Wheaton, IL: Quest Books, 2002

Jung and the Lost Gospels. Wheaton, IL: Quest Books, 1989

Holroyd, Stuart, *The Elements of Gnosticism*. Shaftesbury: Element Books, 1994

The Holy Bible: Revised Standard Version. Oxford University Press, 2005

Jacobs, Alan, *The Essential Gnostic Gospels*. London: Watkins Publishing, 2006

James, M.R., *The Apocryphal New Testament*. Oxford University Press, 1955

Jonas, Hans, *The Gnostic Religion*. Boston: Beacon, 1963

Kasser, R., M. Meyer and G. Wurst (eds), *The Gospel of Judas: From Codex Tchacos*. Washington, DC: National Geographic, 2006

King, C. W., *The Gnostics and Their Remains, Ancient and Medieval*. San Diego: Wizards Bookshelf, 1982

King, Karen L., *The Gospel of Mary of Magdala*. Santa Rosa: Polebridge Press, 2003

   The Secret Revelation of John. Cambridge, MA: Harvard University Press, 2006

   What Is Gnosticism. London: Harvard University Press, 2003

Klimkeit, Hans-Joachim, *Gnosis on the Silk Road: Gnostic Texts from Central Asia*. San Francisco: Harper, 1993

Koester, Helmut, *Ancient Christian Gospels: Their History and Development*. Harrisburg, PA: Trinity Press, 1990

   Introduction to the New Testament in Two Volumes. New York: Walter De Gruyter, 1982

Lacarrière, Jacques, *The Gnostics*. San Francisco: City Lights, 1989

Layton, Bentley, *The Gnostic Scriptures*. New York: Doubleday, 1995

Layton, Bentley (ed.), *Nag Hammadi Codex II, 2–7*: vol. 1. Leiden: Brill, 1989

Leloup, Jean-Yves, *The Gospel of Philip: Jesus, Mary Magdalene, and the Gnosis of Sacred Union*. Rochester, VT: Inner Traditions, 2004

Ludemann, Gerd, and Martina Janssen, *Suppressed Prayers: Gnostic Spirituality in Early Christianity*. PLACE: Trinity Press International, 1998

Lupieri, Edmondo, *The Mandaeans: The Last Gnostics*. Grand Rapids, MI: Eerdmans, 2002

MacDermot, Violet, *The Fall of Sophia: A Gnostic Text on the Redemption of Universal Consciousness*. Great Barrington, MA: Lindisfarne Books, 2001

Martin, Sean, *The Cathars*. Harpenden: Pocket Essentials, 2006

Mead, G.R.S., *Echoes From the Gnosis: Centennial Edition*. Wheaton, ILL: Quest Books, 2006

   Fragments of a Faith Forgotten. Dublin: Bardic Press, 2008

   Gnostic John the Baptizer: Selections from the Mandæan John-

Book, Kila, MT: Kessinger Publishing, reprinted 1993

Pistis Sophia. New York: Dover Books, 2005

Simon Magus: His Philosophy and Teachings. San Diego: The Book Tree, 2003

Merkur, Dan, *Gnosis: An Esoteric Tradition of Mystical Visions and Unions.* New York: SUNY Press, 1993

Meyer, Marvin (ed.), *Ancient Christian Magic.* HarperSanFrancisco, 1994

The Gospel of Thomas: The Hidden Sayings of Jesus. HarperSanFrancisco, 1992

The Unknown Sayings of Jesus. HarperSanFrancisco, 1998

Miller, Robert J. (ed.), *The Complete Gospels.* Sonoma, CA: Polebridge Press, 1992

Morrice, William, *The Hidden Sayings of Jesus.* Peabody, MA: Hendrickson, 1997

Oldenbourg, Zoé, *Massacre at Montségur: A History of the Albigensian Crusade.* London: Phoenix, 1999

O'Shea, Stephen, *The Perfect Heresy: The Revolutionary Life and Death of the Medieval Cathars.* New York: Walker and Co, 2000

Ouspensky, P.D., *In Search of the Miraculous.* London: Routledge & Kegan, 1950

A New Model of the Universe London: Alfred A. Knopf, 1934

Pagels, Elaine, *Adam, Eve and the Serpent.* New York: Random House, 1988

The Gnostic Gospels. New York: Vintage Books, 1981

The Gnostic Paul: Gnostic Exegesis of the Pauline Letters. Philadelphia: Trinity Press, 1992

The Johannine Gospel in Gnostic Exegesis: Heracleon's Commentary on John. Nashville and New York: Abingdon Press, 1973

The Origin of Satan. New York: Random House, 1995

Pagels, Elaine, and Karen L. King, *Reading Judas: The Gospel of Judas and the Shaping of Christianity.* New York: Viking, 2007

Partner, Peter, *The Knights Templar and Their Myth*. Rochester, VT: Destiny Books, 1990

Petrement, Simone, *A Separate God: The Christian Origins of Gnosticism*. San Francisco: Harper, 1990

Plotinus, trans. Stephen MacKenna, *The Enneads*. Harmondsworth: Penguin: 1991

Price, Robert M., *Deconstructing Jesus*. Amherst, NY: Prometheus, 2000

Roberts, Alexander, and James Donaldson (eds), *The Ante-Nicene Fathers in 10 Volumes*. Peabody, MA: Hendrickson Publishers, Inc., 2004

Robinson, James (ed.), *The Nag Hammadi Library in English*. San Francisco: Harper and Row, rev. ed. 1988

Robson, James, *Christ in Islam*. Oregon House, CA: Bardic Press, 2005

Roukema, Riemer, *Gnosis and Faith in Early Christianity*. Harrisberg, PA: Trinity Press, 1999

Rudolph, Kurt, *Gnosis: The Nature & History of Gnosticism*. Oxford University Press, 1984

Runciman, Steven, *The Medieval Manichee: A Study of the Christian Dualist Heresy*. New York: Viking Press, 1961

Salaman, Clement, et al, *The Way of Hermes*. Rochester, VT: Inner Traditions, 2000

Scheemelcher, Wilhelm (ed.), trans. R.McL. Wilson, *New Testament Apocrypha*, vol. 1: *Gospels and Related Writings*. Louisville, KY: Westminster/John Knox Press, rev. ed. 1991

Seymor-Smith, Martin, *Gnosticism: The Path of Inner Knowledge*. HarperSanFrancisco, 1996

Singer, June, *A Gnostic Book of Hours: Keys to Inner Wisdom*. San Francisco: Harper, 1992

Smith, Andrew Phillip, *Gnostic Writings on the Soul: Annotated & Explained*. Woodstock, VT: Skylight Paths, 2006

The Gospel of Philip: Annotated & Explained. Woodstock, VT: Skylight Paths, 2005

The Gospel of Thomas: A New Translation Based On the Inner Meaning. Oregon House, CA: Ulysses Books, 2002

The Lost Sayings of Jesus: Annotated & Explained. Woodstock, VT: Skylight Paths, 2006

Smith, Carl B. II, *No Longer Jews: The Search for Gnostic Origins*. Peabody, MA: Hendrickson, 2004

Smith, Morton, *Jesus the Magician*. New York: Barnes & Noble, 1993

Smoley, Richard, *Forbidden Faith: The Gnostic Legacy from the Gospels to the Da Vinci Code*. New York: HarperCollins, 2006

Stoyanov, Yuri, *The Other God: Dualist Religions from Antiquity to the Cathar Heresy*. New Haven: Yale University Press, rev. ed. 2000

Stroker, William D., *Extracanonical Sayings of Jesus*. Atlanta, GA: Scholars Press, 1989

Turner, John D., 'The Figure of Hecate and Dynamic Emanationism in the Chaldaean Oracles, Sethian Gnosticism and Neoplatonism', in *The Second Century Journal*, 7:4, (1991), pp. 221–32

'The Gnostic Seth', in M. Stone and T. Bergren (eds), *Biblical Figures Outside the Bible*, (Harrisburg, PA: Trinity Press International, 1998), pp. 33–58

'The Gnostic Threefold Path to Enlightenment: The Ascent of Mind and the Descent of Wisdom', in *Novum Testamentum* 22 (1980), pp. 324–51

'Gnosticism and Platonism: The Platonizing Texts from Nag Hammadi in their Relation to Later Platonic Literature', in R.T. Wallis (ed.), *Gnosticism and Neoplatonism*, Studies in Neoplatonism 6. Albany: S.U.N.Y. Press, 1992), pp. 425–59

'Ritual in Gnosticism', in Society of Biblical Literature Seminar Papers, 1994 (Atlanta, GA: Scholars Press, 1994), pp. 136–81

'Sethian Gnosticism: A Literary History', in C.W. Hedrick and R. Hodgson (eds), *Nag Hammadi, Gnosticism and Early Christianity* (Peabody, MA: Hendrickson Publishers, 1986), pp. 55–86

'To See The Light: A Gnostic Appropriation Of Jewish Priestly
Practice and Sapiential and Apocalyptic Visionary Lore', in
R.M. Berchman (ed.), *Mediators of the Divine: Horizons of
Prophecy and Divination on Mediterranean Antiquity* (Florida
Studies in the History of Judaism 163; Atlanta, GA: Scholars
Press, 1998), pp. 63–113

'Typologies of the Sethian Gnostic Literature from Nag
Hammadi', in *Colloque internationale sur les textes de Nag
Hammadi*, Université Laval, 15–22 Sept., 1993 (Louvain and
Quebec: Peeters and Université Laval, 1994), pp. 169–217

Turner, John D., and Anne McGuire (eds.), *The Nag Hammadi
Library after Fifty Years: Proceedings of the 1995 Society of
Biblical Literature Commemoration*, Nag Hammadi and
Manichaean Studies, 44. Leiden: Brill, 1997 (see esp. Martha
Lee Turner, 'On the Coherence of the Gospel According to
Philip', pp. 223–50; Einar Thomassen, 'How Valentinian is the
Gospel of Philip?', pp. 251–79; Elaine Pagels, 'Ritual in the
Gospel of Philip', pp. 280-91)

Turner, Martha Lee, *The Gospel According to Philip: The Sources and
Coherence of an Early Christian Collection,* Nag Hammadi and
Manichaean Studies, 38, Leiden: E.J. Brill, 1996

Valantasis, Richard, *Religions of Late Antiquity in Practice*,
Princeton University Press, 2000

Vrettos, Theodore, *Alexandria: City of the Western Mind*. New York:
The Free Press, 2001

Wakefield, Walter L., and Austin P. Evans, *Heresies of the High
Middle Ages*. New York: Columbia University Press, 1991

Walker, Benjamin, *Gnosticism: Its History and Influence*.
Wellingborough: The Aquarian Press, 1983

Webb, James, *The Harmonious Circle*. Boston: Shambhala, 1987

Weis, René, *The Yellow Cross: The Story of the Last Cathars'
Rebellion Against the Inquisition 1290–1329*. New York: Vintage
Books, 2002

Welburn, Andrew, *Mani, the Angel and the Column of Glory: An
Anthology of Manichean Texts*. Edinburgh: Floris Books, 1998

Williams, Michael A., *Rethinking Gnosticism*. Princeton University Press, 1999

Wilson, R. McL., *The Gospel of Philip*. New York: Harper & Row, 1962

INDEX